Contents

THE PROBLEM OF STERLING

A. R. CONAN

MACMILLAN
London · Melbourne · Toronto

ST MARTIN'S PRESS
New York
1966

MACMILLAN AND COMPANY LTD
Little Essex Street London WC2
also Bombay Calcutta Madras Melbourne
THE MACMILLAN COMPANY OF CANADA LIMITED
70 Bond Street Toronto 2
ST. MARTIN'S PRESS INC
175 Fifth Avenue New York NY 10010

Library of Congress Catalog Card Number 66—21360

PRINTED IN GREAT BRITAIN

CHAPTER ONE

Introduction

i. THE CASE FOR REVIEW

The aim of this work is to analyse the problem of sterling. A new study of a topic which has been widely debated may be thought superfluous but can perhaps be justified. The substance of the problem alters from time to time and thus discussion is sometimes based on obsolescent assumptions: there was, for example, a lengthy time-lag before it was accepted that post-war recovery had invalidated the analysis put forward at the end of the war. Similarly, developments in the overseas sterling area may escape notice even if they involve radical changes: here again the older view of the sterling mechanism (especially for the reserves) no longer accords with fact. Finally, the material for a realistic study has latterly been extended: though still incomplete, the data now available call for revision of opinion on some major points.

For these reasons a critical survey of the problem may be timely. It should help to define the issues in concrete detail and can also be utilised to test the theories which purport to account for the existence of the problem. With the scope of the present study limited to analysis, no specific policy measures or reforms are advocated but an attempt will be made to collate the data needed for the appraisal of policy and to indicate areas where data are lacking.

Although restricted in scope, the task is far from simple because of the multiple factors involved. Sterling as the currency of the United Kingdom responds to changes within that economy but is also responsive to factors originating elsewhere. As the reserve currency of overseas sterling countries, it supports their international payments and at times these transactions may impose an extra burden. Other countries also use sterling for trade or finance and events in the non-sterling world may thus react on the pound. A comprehensive study should not, therefore, be confined to the United Kingdom alone but must cover a wider field.

Intricate problems of this kind can be stated with clarity only if the relevant material is organised as a coherent whole. The treatment adopted here is mainly based on balance of payments data. Such a scheme should allow the evidence to be set out in unified form and will exhibit the factors operative over a given period: it also facilitates analysis by enabling the main elements of the problem to be isolated and their relative magnitudes compared. In places the treatment has been extended by reference to longer-term trends or the record for other countries.

With the plan proposed the basic material will be examined in Chapters Two to Four, while in Chapter Five some provisional results will be stated and an attempt made to put the problem into perspective. Before embarking on a detailed survey, however, the issues may be identified in more general terms.

ii. THE ELEMENTS OF THE PROBLEM

Successive crises for nearly twenty years register the persistence of the problem: it had emerged during the earlier war years and was then alleviated by Lend-Lease arrangements, but at the end of the war became a major concern of economic policy. Its subsequent history can best be approached by reference to conditions as envisaged by policy-planners at that time.

The situation was outlined in an authoritative text prepared for official use in 1945.[1] This appraisal, which comprised an inventory of war losses and evaluated their effects on the balance of payments, listed the critical items. One (which was given great weight) was the loss of the United

[1] Cmd. 6707: *Statistical Material Presented during the Washington Negotiations.*

Kingdom's creditor status implicit in wartime disposals of overseas investments and the accumulation of short-term liabilities. Under such conditions the existing gold reserves seemed inadequate, and this was to remain a source of anxiety: the disparity between reserves and liabilities also occasioned debate on the size of the sterling balances and possible methods of redeeming them. In addition, there were misgivings as to the future trend of the current account: exports had been largely sacrificed during the war while it was accepted that war losses would greatly impair invisible receipts.

The table on p. 4 will serve as a preliminary check on this analysis: at the same time it indicates the limitations of such data as a reliable guide.

Some of the limitations are evident on scrutiny of the current balance. After the initial deficits in 1946–47 (which had been foreseen) a surplus was maintained until 1951 (it will be noted that the figures do not register the 1949 crisis). Post-war recovery was consolidated during the 1950s: excluding 1951 (a special case) there was a deficit only in 1955 and a substantial cumulative surplus for the decade as a whole (again, the figures for 1957, when there was a comfortable surplus, do not register the crisis of that year). On the whole the record could be accounted good yet fifteen years after the end of the war, at the beginning of the 1960s, the deficits reappeared.

The figures for the reserves are not readily reconcilable with this trend. In 1947, with a current deficit of £450 million, the reserves fell by only £150 million, and in 1951 the loss of reserves was again appreciably less than the deficit; in 1955 the loss was much greater than the deficit but the effect of the very large shortfall in 1960 cannot be discerned. Apart from the data for specific years, the evidence generally is to the same effect: the cumulative surplus for the 1950s exceeded £1000 million while the increase in the reserves was under £400 million.

The trend for the sterling balances appears to negative any suggestion that the reserves rose slowly because the current surplus was used to reduce liabilities. At the beginning of the 1950s these were shown at over £3000 million (some £400 million below the end-war figure despite a cumulative deficit for the years 1946–49): at the end of 1959

THE UNITED KINGDOM BALANCE OF PAYMENTS: A TWENTY-YEAR SURVEY

£ million

	Current Account	Gold Reserves	Sterling Balances
1946	−295	664	3610
1947	−442	512	3498
1948	7	457	3152
1949	38	603	3143
1950	297	1178	3483
1951	−419	834	3577
1952	170	659	3219
1953	151	899	3493
1954	121	986	3703
1955	−157	757	3576
1956	209	799	3422
1957	216	812	3273
1958	330	1096	3353
1959	132	977	3507
1960	−273	1154	3883
1961	−14	1185	3546
1962	93	1002	2937†
1963	105	949	3071†
1964	−412	827	3060†
1965	−16*	997	2866†

* January–June. † New series.

Note. Gold Reserves and Sterling Balances as at end of year except for 1965, which are mid-year. In 1949 the reserves were written up after devaluation. The new series for the sterling balances starting in 1962 includes a total for that year some £500 million less than the old series.

the total again exceeded £3500 million (despite the cumulative surplus). Moreover, as the reserves (in terms of dollars) were hardly greater than at the end of the war, it could be said that there was no real improvement in the reserve ratio.

On the post-war record, therefore, the current account proves unreliable as a guide to the strength of sterling: weakness has not always coincided with a deficit while little of the surplus earned during the 1950s seems to have been added to the reserves. Any theory which relates the strength of sterling to the state of the current account must accordingly be suspect. Perhaps better guidance can be obtained from movements in the reserves or in the ratio of reserves to liabilities but if these indicators are used, it should be emphasised that they reflect not merely the current balance but other factors also.

One such factor is the overseas sterling area. The current transactions of this sector have a double impact on the reserve ratio. As its sterling balances are the external assets of member countries, the level of these balances fluctuates in accordance with the net outturn for the countries concerned. The level of the reserves is likewise affected since the overseas sterling area deposits receipts of non-sterling currencies (and newly-mined gold) in the central pool and draws on it for non-sterling expenditures. In so far as the strength of the pound depends on the state of the reserves (or the reserve ratio) a full analysis must cover the transactions not of the United Kingdom only but of the whole sterling area.

Yet another factor must be introduced to complete the analysis. The reserves and the sterling balances register both current transactions and also capital movements. Since the war imports of long-term capital into overseas sterling countries have sustained their London balances at a high level: such imports from non-sterling sources into the whole sterling area have replenished the reserves. At times, too, movements of short-term capital into or out of the United Kingdom have involved corresponding changes in the reserves. The magnitude of all these capital movements has made them a dominant feature of the post-war scene.

The foregoing summary exemplifies the intricacy of the problem and also suggests the lines of a realistic treatment. In the first instance the United Kingdom current balance must be analysed in order to determine the repercussions of wartime losses or post-war failures. This can lead to a critical review of the main theories bearing on the sterling problem and of the policies adopted to deal with it. If these theories and policies seem inadequate, further attempts must be made to identify other relevant factors: the examination should extend to the overseas sterling area as well as to the United Kingdom itself. The results of the full survey can then be summarised for the period as a whole.

The following chapter will trace the development of the United Kingdom current account as the prerequisite for a review of theory and policy.

CHAPTER TWO

The Record for the Current Balance

i. POST-WAR RECOVERY, 1946–50

The appraisal of the post-war problem drawn up for the United States loan negotiations in 1945 may now be examined in more detail. This paper set out the effects of the war and the causes of the prospective deficit under the following heads:

Loss of Exports. 'British export trade shrank to less than one-third of its pre-war volume and, despite some recovery . . . a period of acute difficulty must be faced until the reconversion of industry, the release of manpower and the recovery and expansion of export markets have begun to result in a substantial flow of exports.'

Loss of Overseas Investments. 'It is estimated that the net income from overseas investments in 1945 will be less than half that received in 1938. This reflects the extensive liquidation of foreign securities, the repatriation of loans by overseas debtors, and the increased payments to holders of sterling debts caused by the heavy war expenditure which the UK has had to incur overseas.'

Loss of Shipping. 'More than half of the pre-war tonnage of British merchant shipping was lost during the war. . . . Until the fleet has been expanded and carrying trades abandoned in the war have been recovered, the net income available from shipping services to supplement UK purchasing power abroad will be greatly below pre-war level.'

The Increase of Overseas Debt. '. . . The UK has incurred huge debts in the form of accumulated sterling balances. . . . There will inevitably remain heavy commitments to be met overseas. . . . Thus apart from the repayment of the war debts a further substantial, though temporary, burden of current expenditure abroad has to be sustained. . . .'[1]

[1] Cmd. 6707.

A forecast of the probable trend for the current balance provided for a deficit of some £750 million in 1946 followed by one of £500 million in 1947–48 taken together, with 'some more modest deficiency in 1949 and 1950'. Thus for the first five post-war years the official appraisal envisaged a cumulative deficit 'which may well be £1250 million or even higher'.

The appraisal (with the forecast based on it) was an attempt to fix the magnitude of the payments problem. At the time it was not easy to predict the probable outturn or assess the relative weight of the different factors involved and the results should accordingly be checked against the record. This can be done by reference to the table below:

COMPONENTS OF THE CURRENT BALANCE

£ million

	Trade Balance	Other Items*	Government Account	Total
1938	−302	248	−16	−70
1946	−162	190	−323	−295
1947	−414	121	−149	−442
1948	−190	273	−76	7
1949	−131	308	−139	38
1950	−136	569	−136	297

* Excluding Government.

The table shows that the problem developed contrary to expectations. The visible trade balance responded satisfactorily: the loss of exports was soon made good while imports were strictly controlled. Even for 1946–47 the adverse balance averaged only £300 million per annum (in monetary terms no more than in 1938 and in real terms much less) while for 1949–50 the average was less than half the pre-war figure (very much less if adjusted for higher price levels). On the whole, therefore, the crises of the immediate post-war years cannot be attributed to a deterioration in the trade balance.

It is also clear that invisible receipts (on private account) suffered no appreciable reduction as a result of the war. In 1946 the net total was only about £50 million smaller than in 1938 (a negligible reduction) while by 1948 the former level had been regained and by 1950 receipts were twice the pre-war figure: although for a brief period there was a slight fall in income from overseas investments, shipping earnings rose sharply. (It can of course be said that in the earlier post-war years the total was in real terms smaller than before the war but this is to bring in as an additional factor the world-wide rise in prices.)

The official analysis was therefore misconceived in so far as it based the prospective deficit on the factors specified above: the results show a *surplus* for all items on private account in 1946 as compared with a deficit in 1938. The main impact of the war appeared not in the ordinary categories of the current balance but in the novel item of Government expenditure overseas: the debit under this head, negligible before the war, imposed at first a severe strain with corresponding relief when the burden was eased.

Taking all categories together the record was good, with a deficit for a very short time (in 1946–47): this deficit had been accepted as inevitable in view of the transition from war to peace conditions and policy was planned accordingly. Later, there was a near-balance in 1948–49 and a large surplus in 1950. The outcome for the first post-war quinquennium was thus much better than had been forecast: the cumulative deficit was under £400 million (one-third of the estimated figure) and nearly all of it was incurred just after the war. On these results the current balance seemed in better shape than before the war since in the quinquennium 1934–38 a surplus was recorded only once (1935).

It may be objected that even in the recovery period (here taken as no more than five years) the favourable trend was broken by balance of payments crises on two occasions, in 1947 and 1949. But the objection can be overcome: although crises were encountered during the early post-war years they did not reflect strains in the current balance as such.

On the first occasion the figures seem to justify the

suggestion of a deterioration in the current account sufficient to cause a crisis. In fact, however, the deficit for 1947 as for 1946 (when there was no crisis) was foreseen: post-war policy was based on the assumption that until exports could be restored it would be necessary to tolerate a deficit and dollar loans were negotiated to tide over this period. It cannot be said, therefore, that recovery in the current balance was checked by the 1947 crisis.

The evidence becomes clearer for the 1949 crisis. Here, again, there is no sign of a set-back in the current account: there was now an appreciable surplus for the first time since the war. The events which occasioned the devaluation of the pound cannot be attributed to a failure of the current balance but must have had other origins. Thus, the concept of surplus or deficit (on this basis) is inadequate as an explanation of crisis conditions.

The possibility of crises co-existing with a favourable trend for the current balance testifies to the complexity of the sterling problem while even the make-up of the balance itself is far from simple. Inspection of the data will show how the deficit of £300 million recorded in 1946 was transformed into a surplus of the same amount in 1950. The transformation (a turn-round of some £600 million) was *not* effected via the trade account: despite the rapid recovery in exports, there was in both years an import surplus of approximately £150 million. The record for visible trade was in contrast with that for the invisible items: here a deficit of nearly £150 million was replaced by a surplus of almost £450 million.

As a case-study in the structure of the current account the results are noteworthy. For this quinquennium at any rate the trade balance was relatively insignificant: the surplus was derived from invisibles. (Further analysis reveals the extent to which the increase in net invisible receipts was dependent on a reduction in Government expenditure, now a major determinant of the total.) There is thus no correlation between visible trade and the current surplus: in 1950, for example, the trade balance was virtually the same as in

1949 but the surplus rose from less than £50 million in the former year to almost £300 million in the latter. The contrast between the visible and the invisible categories is instructive as early evidence of a trend which proved persistent.

From the record, therefore, it can be seen that the official appraisal of the post-war problem was defective in overestimating the size of the probable deficit and attributing it to factors which proved to be of minor significance. At several points the magnitudes involved were misjudged. Even at the outset the deficit on trade account was quite small and the reduction in net invisibles on private account relatively modest. The forecast was also erroneous in underestimating the rapidity with which recovery could be effected: in fact exports were quickly restored (and expanded) while invisibles on private account had fully recovered as early as 1948. With the initial assumptions falsified, the whole basis of the exercise proved unsound.

Despite the evidence which soon became available, this faulty appraisal was for years uncritically accepted. It was widely believed that there was a chronic deficit at a time when the current balance was on the whole in surplus; it was generally assumed that the trade balance was highly adverse although the import surplus was relatively small and that invisible receipts had fallen heavily while in fact they had risen sharply; the state of the Government account was seldom noted. So long as these views were prevalent, confidence in the pound could hardly be restored.

Under such conditions, too, diagnosis was likely to go astray. As late as 1951 Robbins asserted[1] that since the war there had been 'a persistent shortage of foreign exchange' but did not explain how it arose in the absence of a current deficit: he also linked the earliest crises with a deterioration in the current balance. The record hardly confirms an interpretation along these lines since in 1947 the planned deficit was fully covered by loans while in 1949 there was a

[1] L. Robbins: *The Balance of Payments* (Stamp Memorial Lecture, 1951).

surplus. A realistic analysis must therefore ascribe the crises to factors other than weakness in the current account.

ii. THE 1950S AND AFTER

A realistic analysis based on firm data is also needed to interpret the history of sterling during the 1950s. This period may reasonably claim separate treatment as a new phase in the post-war record. The situation just after the war was exceptional and transient: during the 1950s, as the war receded, an approach to normal conditions could be postulated, while as compared with the brief recovery period the decade affords a more extended view of the problem. The behaviour of the current balance during these years (and in the early 1960s) should therefore be the main object of study.

At the outset a large surplus gave a misleading impression of security. The devaluation of sterling had been intended to finalise reconstruction and aid future expansion but once more the official appraisal seemed at fault and policy ineffective: as early as 1951 the current balance was again heavily in deficit.

The origins of this deficit will be discussed later (pp. 55–6) and here it need only be said that although the incidence of the crisis was severe, there is little evidence of deep-seated or persistent disequilibrium: the deficit was occasioned by a political emergency in the Far East and soon subsided. Thereafter, for the greater part of the 1950s, the current account showed a favourable trend although on two occasions (1955 and 1959) this was checked by the relaxation of import controls. Apart from these set-backs there was marked progress: the average annual surplus (recorded transactions) rose from approximately £75 million for the years 1952–55 to three times that figure for 1956–59. The true surplus may have been somewhat greater.[1]

[1] The unidentified balancing item showed a cumulative credit total of nearly £400 million for the eight years 1952–59, i.e. an average of £50 million per annum.

THE UNITED KINGDOM CURRENT BALANCE, 1950–64

£ million

	Exports	Imports	Trade Balance	Investment Income Cr.	Investment Income Dr.	Investment Income Net	Shipping Income (Net)	Government Account	Other Items	Total
1950	2254	2390	−136	271	112	159	141	−136	269	297
1951	2752	3501	−749	305	158	147	132	−150	201	−419
1952	2769	3048	−279	500	248	252	134	−54	117	170
1953	2683	2927	−244	493	266	227	88	−58	138	151
1954	2785	2989	−204	539	290	249	36	−126	166	121
1955	3073	3386	−313	516	343	173	−30	−139	152	−157
1956	3377	3324	53	569	342	227	−48	−172	149	209
1957	3509	3538	−29	579	334	245	7	−147	140	216
1958	3407	3375	32	679	389	290	43	−224	189	330
1959	3522	3638	−116	659	396	263	16	−233	202	132
1960	3733	4137	−404	676	438	238	−32	−286	211	−273
1961	3892	4041	−149	676	424	252	−28	−338	249	−14
1962	3994	4092	−98	743	419	324	−12	−362	241	93
1963	4287	4366	−79	828	441	387	−12	−382	191	105
1964	4471	5005	−534	866	461	405	−25	−439	181	−412

Source: United Kingdom balance of payments statements (figures for 1950–51 may not be fully comparable with those for subsequent years).

The trend reflected an even more marked improvement for visible trade. At the beginning of the decade the import surplus was as much as £450 million per annum (average of 1950 and 1951, a good and a bad year) but it soon disappeared: on the average for 1956–59 exports and imports were in approximate balance. To attain such a balance was in itself remarkable. With price levels approximately three times as high as before the war, the pre-war import surplus (if the volume of trade were unchanged) would have amounted to about £1000 million. The first task was to eliminate this massive deficit and that was effected during the 1950s.

At a later stage it will be necessary to examine the record for visible trade since the trend must raise doubts whether the behaviour of the trade account during this decade is consistent with the view that chronic inflation was a valid diagnosis for the balance of payments problem. But it may be noted here that the virtual elimination of the import surplus (if permanent) would represent a major structural change in the current balance as equilibrium would no longer depend on receipts from invisibles.

The favourable outturn for visible trade was not matched by comparable results for other components of the current balance. On the contrary, the two main categories showed signs of deterioration: between 1952 and 1959 there was no expansion in receipts from invisibles on private account while the debit on Government account rose sharply.

The check to expansion in the former category was unforeseen. Earlier, there had been a rapid recovery and by 1952 net receipts under this head were in monetary terms perhaps twice as great as before the war. Yet no further growth occurred during the 1950s and the total tended to fall. One reason for this set-back was the failure of shipping receipts, which involved a loss of over £100 million per annum. More serious was the growth of large debits on investment income account: as a result of these debits, net investment income in 1959 was not appreciably greater than in 1952.

Poor results from the investment income account were a real weakness since it was now, with the failure of shipping income, the only major credit.[1] Moreover, wartime losses had been made good by new capital exports: before the end of the 1940s gross investment income had regained the pre-war level and by 1952 was put at £500 million, compared with the pre-war estimate of under £250 million. Nor was this all: with further heavy exports of capital during the 1950s there was a continued expansion, gross receipts reaching nearly £700 million before the end of the decade. Thus, even with some allowance for possible understatement of earlier estimates, the total was in monetary terms about three times as great as before the war.

Despite this impressive total, however, the investment income account as a whole was unsatisfactory because heavier receipts were largely offset by payments due. Before the war the total for these payments was estimated at under £50 million per annum; by 1959 it had reached £400 million.

The debit comprised several distinct items. One, of minor importance, is the interest payable on the dollar loans received from Canada and the United States at the end of the war: although the capital sum is large, the annual interest is under £40 million. Another, of greater significance, derives from the sterling balances created during the war. The amount needed for the service of the balances was relatively small during the earlier post-war years (about £30 million per annum) but naturally increased when interest rates were raised in 1951: in the latter part of the 1950s it averaged over £100 million per annum. The debit on portfolio investment is still small (£74 million in 1964) but profits on externally-owned direct investment may be as much as £200 million per annum.

These items constitute in the aggregate a heavy burden: although credits continued to rise, the increase in debits (mostly during the 1950s) has severely restricted net investment income.

[1] The composite 'other items' yielded an appreciable net credit.

The deterioration for invisibles on private account was untimely because it coincided with a similar trend for the Government account: between the beginning and the end of the 1950s this debit became once more a major factor in the current balance. After the earlier post-war years it had been much reduced, falling from £300 million in 1946 to hardly more than £50 million in 1952; subsequently, higher expenditure overseas with a reduction in offsetting credits brought the total to nearly £250 million in 1959.

With a reduction in net invisible receipts, the surplus from the current balance during the 1950s was less than might have been expected by reference to visible trade alone: the improvement in the trade balance was neutralised by the failure of shipping income, the new debit for investment income and the debit on Government account. Again, certain magnitudes must be emphasised. It has already been seen that the visible trade account had to eliminate an import surplus which at post-war prices amounted to some £1000 million per annum; now it can be seen that in addition the current balance had to absorb new debits which by the early 1960s were not far short of another £1000 million per annum (as well as the loss of shipping income): that task, too, was accomplished.

On the whole, the results for the 1950s hardly imply the existence of any underlying malaise in the *economy* (although the unfavourable trend for invisibles in the *current balance* was a new adverse factor). It would accordingly be reasonable to maintain that in this period (as in the earlier post-war years) the current balance as such did not prove intractable: the post-war recovery was consolidated, culminating in a large surplus for 1958. The Radcliffe Committee expressed satisfaction with the results and noting that the record was much more favourable than before the war, it concluded as follows:

The fact that there has been a substantial surplus on current account during the past ten years suggests that there has been no fundamental lack of balance in the United Kingdom's trading position . . . exports and imports have roughly kept pace with one another: on the whole the margin between the two has tended to widen and leave a rather more favourable balance. The repeated exchange crises have not been due therefore to any failure on the part of the United Kingdom to pay her way. . . .[1]

When the Report of the Committee was issued in 1959 signs of change had already become visible. Although a final judgment would be premature, it would probably be right to treat the 1960s as a third phase in the history of the post-war sterling problem. A fifteen-year period since the end of the war should have allowed ample scope for making good war losses but ten years after recovery seemed assured the problem of sterling was still unsolved: during the first quinquennium of the 1960s the current balance was heavily in deficit on two occasions.

Certain features of this new phase may be noted. One was the more volatile character of the trade balance due to the fact that imports could now vary much more freely than formerly. After the large surplus in 1958 it was judged that the balance of payments was buoyant and import controls were accordingly discarded. As a result imports rose sharply in 1960 (when the total was some 25 per cent greater than in 1958). The same phenomenon recurred (for other reasons) in 1964 when imports rose by 15 per cent as compared with a year earlier.

It was unfortunate that at a time when the trade balance became more sensitive than formerly, the invisible account should deteriorate further. At the beginning of the decade net invisible receipts fell to negligible proportions, the total for 1960–61 being well under £150 million per annum as compared with £450 million ten years earlier. The shipping account, for the first time, was consistently in deficit and, although there was some improvement in net investment income, the reverse was true for the Government account: at the end of the 1950s the debit was still under £250 million but by 1964 had increased twofold.

[1] *Committee on the Working of the Monetary System* (Cmnd. 827): Report, para 633.

Thus, in contrast with the 1950s, there was a continuing weakness in the invisibles at a time when the trade balance was liable to come under pressure. This in itself might be taken as marking a new phase. In the recovery period there was a favourable trend for both the trade balance and the invisibles; during the 1950s an improvement in the former coincided with a deterioration in the latter. Now both categories developed an adverse trend simultaneously.

The recurrence of weakness in the new phase was interpreted as further evidence that the problem of sterling was still unsolved. Yet there was still no accepted diagnosis for the problem and little agreement on a practicable solution. A summary of the main attempts at diagnosis and of the policies adopted or advocated will be given in the following chapter. Here, however, it will be useful to take some points arising out of the post-war record as a whole.

iii. NOTES ON THE POST-WAR RECORD

The evidence set out in the two preceding sections comprises only part of the data relevant to the sterling problem but will serve for a preliminary analysis. Before undertaking this analysis, however, some points should be clarified.

The first point concerns the interpretation of the evidence. In generalised statements the post-war history of sterling is often presented as a succession of crises in the current balance but this view is unacceptable. The conditions which occasioned crises were not invariably the same and the crises manifested themselves in diverse forms.

To determine the actual number of all these crises it is first necessary to decide whether they are best indicated by a failure in the current balance or a fall in the reserves. No doubt should arise where both phenomena appear simultaneously but for some years (1949 and 1952) the current balance was in surplus and the reserves fell while for others (1946 and 1960) the reserves rose although the current balance was in deficit.

In fact neither 1946 nor 1960 was at the time regarded as

a crisis year, despite a large short-fall on current account: it may thus be inferred that a current deficit is not necessarily embarrassing. On the other hand, a heavy fall in the reserves has invariably been associated with crisis.

The years commonly taken as crises include two in the 1940s (1947 and 1949), three in the 1950s (1951, 1955 and 1957) and (so far) two in the 1960s (1961 and 1964). This gives a total of seven in twenty years but it seems unrealistic to treat 1947 (any more than 1946) as a failure of the current balance. It will be found that there were current balance crises on three occasions (1951, 1955 and perhaps 1964): crises occasioned by a drain on the reserves not directly related to the current balance occurred more frequently as that phenomenon appeared in 1947, 1949, 1957 and 1961.

At the outset therefore it can be established that the current balance is merely one possible element in a crisis situation: other possibilities must not be excluded. It is also evident from the record that although at intervals breaks in the trend interrupted the longer-term development, the current balance itself was generally favourable both in the earlier recovery period and during the 1950s (judgment on the 1960s should perhaps be suspended until a clearer picture emerges). The intermittent deficits were on occasion substantial but their significance should not be over-emphasised.

First, there is no reason why exports and imports should move exactly together and every likelihood that an upsurge in the latter will not be matched by an equivalent increase in the former. For a country heavily dependent on imports of raw materials, a rise in imports must normally precede a rise in exports (unless stocks are drawn down): furthermore, in value terms, a large increase in imports (of food as well as raw materials) may be due not to domestic factors but to higher world commodity prices (as in 1951). Import trends of this kind can readily be countered in a country such as the United States where the export sector of the economy is relatively small but the adjustment is not so easy in the

United Kingdom where extensive reallocation of resources is needed to evoke an appropriate response from exports.

Next, the magnitudes should be seen in perspective. Even in the exceptional case of 1951 the adverse trade balance was in real terms smaller than in 1938 (when there was no crisis); in 1960 and again in 1964 the adverse balance of £400–500 million compared with the 1938 figure (revalued at current prices) of approximately £1000 million. Such comparisons at least imply that in these crises the trade balance did not register an unparalleled deficit.

Finally, it should be recognised that the statistical evidence for 'crisis years' is mainly based on artificial classifications. The conventional twelve-month period for a balance-sheet of debits and credits is arbitrary: a six-month or a twenty-four-month period would be equally valid. In some cases it may be even more suitable, especially if a particular factor were favourable one year and unfavourable the next. In 1950, for example, import volume was restricted to the 1949 level while exports rose by over 10 per cent; in 1951 there was no increase in export volume but import volume rose by over 10 per cent. With controls operated in this way the two years taken together (giving an average deficit of hardly more than £50 million per annum) may represent the underlying trend better than the large surplus of 1950 and the large deficit of 1951.

The same applies when the relaxation of import control occasions heavy imports which are stock-piled. In such cases the deficit is more apparent than real since by drawing on these stocks a further increase in imports can be avoided for a time: a better measure would be a three-year average including the first year with restricted imports, the next with free imports at a high rate and a third with imports at a more normal rate. On that basis the average for 1954–56 works out at a surplus of over £50 million per annum. In some cases where the movement into stocks is prolonged (as in 1960–61) a wider bracket may be preferable: the results for the years 1959–62 show that over the period as a whole there was a near-balance in the current account.

With this approach the general trend may well prove a better guide to the state of the current balance than intermittent deficits. Although these are commonly taken as indicative of disequilibrium, the diagnosis cannot be accepted without more stringent proof and in some cases the evidence seems inconsistent with such a hypothesis. The reduction of the adverse trade balance between 1948 and 1950, with an increasing surplus on current account, hardly denotes a build-up of pressures which erupted in 1951; much later, in 1965, the trend which asserted itself during the early months of the year suggests that the deficit which persisted throughout 1964 was due to exceptional and transient conditions. Moreover, the fact that the deficits broke a generally favourable trend implies that they were sparked off by extraneous causes: deep-seated disequilibrium would be more likely to show in a gradual deterioration of the current balance over a period of years. Thus, occasional (as opposed to persistent) deficits are not necessarily symptoms of an underlying malaise.

When the crisis years are put into perspective, it seems reasonable to focus attention mainly on the general trend for the current balance over a period. Here a further complication becomes apparent since it has been found that the trend for the balance itself is the resultant of two diverse factors, visible trade and the invisibles, which may act in opposite directions.

The record as analysed earlier in this chapter brings out the significance of the invisible items. In the light of the evidence it is incorrect to regard them as subordinate to visible trade, fulfilling a merely ancillary function in providing cover for the import surplus. Post-war experience demands that they should be assigned a more prominent and active role: it was primarily the invisibles which floated the current balance into surplus during the recovery period while subsequently they restricted the surplus to a figure much lower than might otherwise have been reached. On this evidence the trend for visible trade only is inadequate when appraising the state of the current balance: a full appraisal should therefore cover both categories.

It cannot, however, be assumed as a matter of course that visible trade and the invisibles always develop independently. To some extent at least the buoyancy of the trade balance during the 1950s *may* have reflected the deterioration of the invisibles. This possibility deserves examination.

The link between visible trade and the invisibles is clearest for the Government account. Where official grants or loans are tied to United Kingdom goods there is *prima facie* a response from exports, although the response may be less than the amount of the aid if the recipient country would in any event have taken from the United Kingdom at least some of the exports thus financed. For expenditure on troops and other overseas payments the impact is likely to be slight since the expenditure will be mainly on goods and services purchased abroad for local use.

The United States as a matter of policy has maintained a close relationship between the Government account and exports: about 10 per cent of total exports can be financed by Government through Aid or defence expenditure. If the same proportion held good for the United Kingdom it could be said that the Government debit did not impose any considerable strain on external payments but the two cases are not analogous: the United Kingdom, for example, does not hold any large stocks of surplus commodities earmarked for export under Aid Programmes while its defence expenditure overseas has not been covered by orders for armaments to any significant extent. It thus seems probable that the Government account is only to a minor extent offset by a concomitant increase in exports.

If this conclusion be accepted, little weight can be attached to the argument that a reduction in the Government debit would have adverse effects on exports. Nor does such an argument seem justified by the record: it is certainly not borne out by the figures for the years 1946–50 when the debit was severely curtailed and exports remained buoyant.[1]

A further instance of possible inter-dependence between the visible and the invisible items arises for the investment income account. It is generally accepted that capital exports not only yield a return in the form of investment income but also tend to stimulate visible exports. The reverse may be true of capital imports and as there is now a large annual debit for interest, profits and dividends, the probable reaction on the trade balance should be examined.

In so far as the debit during the earlier post-war years represented interest on the sterling balances there was perhaps some offset in the form of larger exports since the countries which owned these balances could import freely from the United Kingdom (although they would in any case have imported a good deal from that source and the balances were utilised also for imports from other sources). Now probably the greater part of the debit represents profits earned by direct investment in the United Kingdom (mostly of post-war origin) and the net effect of this investment is in question.

The reaction is usually obscure. Although United States companies operating in the United Kingdom may contribute to exports by selling part of their output abroad, there will be no *net* contribution if the exports are at the expense of British firms. The likelihood of such competition points to the contrast between external investment in a primary-producing country (for the development of natural resources) or in an under-developed country (for industrialisation) and investment in a country like the United Kingdom which has no unused natural resources and is already industrialised.

On the other hand, if direct investment in the United

[1] It should be made clear that the Government debit as shown in the official estimates for the current account does not include expenditure on military equipment bought abroad (nor of course loan Aid). Military expenditure accounts for about 60 per cent of the total shown, and grant Aid for about 20 per cent.

Kingdom enables imports to be reduced, there should be some gain (although allowance must be made for higher imports of raw materials) but the gain may be limited because imports of capital normally involve also an increase in imports of capital goods. The possible magnitude of such an increase can be broadly indicated. Expenditure on plant and equipment by United States firms operating in the United Kingdom now amounts to some £250 million per annum. If that sum represents for the most part expenditure on capital goods imported from the United States it would largely explain the higher imports of manufactures (especially machine tools) recorded in recent years: it would also account for much of the adverse trade balance.

The resultant of all these factors can hardly be determined with precision. The official American view is that post-war exports of capital have in general tended to improve the United States trade balance; since imports of capital into the United Kingdom have been mainly from the United States, this view (if valid) would tell against the suggestion that an improvement in the United Kingdom trade balance is to be set against the debit in the investment income account. On the contrary, it seems quite possible that these capital imports have worked against the creation of a trade surplus at a time when the service of the investment burdened the invisibles.

Although any conclusion must be provisional, it seems unlikely that either Government overseas expenditure or the debit for investment income has been or will be offset by a concomitant increase in exports: the view that the post-war expansion in exports was not dependent on such stimuli is perhaps corroborated by the record for the recovery period when there was a rapid expansion in exports although the former was of diminishing importance and the latter not yet operative.

On the whole, therefore, there seems no reason to doubt the reality (or the significance) of structural changes in the current balance as compared with pre-war. To recapitulate:

(*a*) The virtual elimination of the traditional large import surplus (in normal years or on an average for normal and abnormal years) is by itself a striking innovation: if a balance can be secured by visible trade only, the invisibles are otiose.

(*b*) Net receipts from invisibles on private account (all current items) at approximately £600 million are in monetary terms more than twice as great as before the war (were it not for the new debit on investment account, the total would be about £1000 million). Thus, with a negligible import surplus (in normal years) there should be a very substantial surplus in the current balance.

(*c*) Another innovation is the huge debit on Government account (now £450 million net) which at present absorbs most of the invisible receipts on private account. As a determinant of the final outturn the magnitude of this category should not be under-estimated: for the years 1959–63 the adverse trade balance involved a cumulative debit of £850 million while the debit on Government account amounted to £1600 million.

The new pattern has implications for analysis and policy. With a complex balance of payments structure a simple theory cannot account for fluctuations in the current balance: inflation, for example, may operate as a disequilibrating factor in the trade balance but is irrelevant to an increase in the debit on Government account. Again, export performance may be judged satisfactory by reference to earlier standards but inadequate if countered by a simultaneous increase for invisible debits. A complex balance of payments structure affords scope for diverse origins of disequilibrium.

In the policy field likewise, the new pattern complicates the problem. A primitive model with the current account dependent on an equivalence of exports and imports would permit control by methods such as deflation or devaluation but for other categories the traditional controls are likely to be inappropriate. Investment income payable abroad may not be fully amenable to deflationary policy while such a policy would be wholly ineffective in reducing the Government debit (which is dependent primarily on political decisions). Furthermore, if it were proposed to devalue the pound (as against other currencies generally) any prospective gain for the trade balance would have to be set against the certainty of an increase for the Government debit. The relative magnitude of these items enters into the final decision and thus the comparison imposes a choice of priorities: is policy to be aimed at the major or the minor debits?

The analysis so far suggests that post-war changes in the structure of the current balance bear directly on the problem of sterling. The following chapter will utilise the results in examining the origins of the problem and appraising the policies adopted to deal with it.

CHAPTER THREE

Diagnosis and Treatment

Since the end of the war there has been prolonged debate as to the nature of the sterling problem and from time to time different theories have been put forward to account for its emergence or persistence. Here three main theories will be examined.

On one view the post-war problem was attributable to wartime losses: this view was supported by the evidence derived from the war years. On another view the trouble was due to international disequilibrium expressed in a dollar shortage. But perhaps most often inflation has been accepted as the basic trouble. (Latterly, this notion has been formulated in the sense that the growth of the economy involves some degree of strain on the current balance.)

All these theories relate primarily to the current account and to some extent each arose out of contemporary conditions. The emphasis on wartime losses was natural at the end of the war when they were first assessed and thus given prominence. Later, as these losses were made good, other factors such as the dollar problem and inflation came to the fore. Later still, the emergence of a fully-stretched economy focused attention on its special problems.

Each theory suggested a corresponding policy as a remedy. First, given wartime losses, it was proposed to restore the current balance by a massive expansion in exports. Next, in 1949, came the decision to seek a definitive solution of the dollar problem through the devaluation of sterling. Not long afterwards, the use of Bank rate in 1951 implied the adoption of deflationary policy. Ten years later, in 1961, it was decided that an incomes policy was needed as a corrective for the strains attendant on growth.

With the data now available the validity of these theories can be tested more effectively than was possible when they were put forward: in addition, the record will not only indicate whether the remedies adopted were appropriate but will also show whether they were successful.

i. WAR LOSSES AND THE EXPORT TARGET

The diagnosis in the White Paper issued at the end of the war has already been questioned in tracing the course of the current balance. Primarily, criticism may be based on the defective forecast. At least for the earlier years there was misplaced emphasis on the prospective trend for exports, investment income and shipping earnings: the forecasts for these categories were not in fact fulfilled. On the other hand there was little emphasis on the Government account which eventually proved to be far more onerous.

The diagnosis can be further tested by applying it to the first post-war crises, those of 1947 and 1949. In neither case can it account for crisis conditions.

Each crisis manifested itself in falling reserves but this phenomenon was for the most part unconnected with the United Kingdom: on both occasions the drain on the reserves originated elsewhere.

It is true that in 1947 the United Kingdom's dollar balance (current account) was heavily adverse (to the extent of 2000 million dollars) but as large loans had earlier been arranged to cover it, the deficit was not embarrassing: with the proceeds of the loans (3000 million dollars) the United Kingdom contributed approximately 1000 million dollars to the central reserves. The drain on the reserves must thus be attributed to other factors. The overseas sterling area was now in deficit on dollar account to the extent of almost 1000 million dollars (after taking credit for gold sales to the United Kingdom) while in 1946 there had been a small net surplus; in addition, the introduction of convertibility involved a further loss of reserves through the conversion of official balances held in London. The evidence thus affords no support for the view that the outflow from the reserves which necessitated the suspension of convertibility reflected weakness in the United Kingdom.

A similar conclusion is applicable to the next crisis, in 1949. By this time the United Kingdom current account had been brought into balance, with a surplus of nearly £50 million for the year before taking credit for grants received under the European Recovery Programme (the surplus would probably have been larger had these grants not been available). Any pressure on the reserves therefore cannot have derived from the current balance as such but must be explained by reference to other factors.

As in the earlier crisis there was a heavy fall in the reserves: between January and September 1949 the declared total fell by about 500 million dollars and the true loss was much greater. To some extent this reflected a deterioration in the dollar balance of the sterling area as a whole: for the April–June quarter the adverse trade balance with the United States and Canada was at an annual rate of 1750 million dollars (as against 1100 millions for the year 1948) with the deterioration evident for both the United Kingdom and the overseas sector. There was also during the spring and summer a speculative outflow of capital to the dollar area based on the belief that sterling would be devalued: in the July–September quarter this outflow may have been at an annual rate of over 500 million dollars.

Again, therefore, the operative factors are to be found not in the current balance of the United Kingdom but in the dollar balance of the sterling area on both current and capital account. With such evidence it is not easy to maintain that devaluation was necessary because of poor performance by the United Kingdom economy or because of the war losses detailed in the White Paper.

Criticism of the war losses approach does not, however, imply that the White Paper can be omitted from any survey of the sterling problem. For two reasons it must rank as a basic text. First, it gave an official appraisal of the problem and thus reflected the views of those who were involved in policy-making at that time: the risk here was that if the basis on which policy was framed proved insecure, policy measures were not likely to be effective. Secondly, as an official (and therefore authoritative) analysis it created the notion (at home and abroad) that the sterling problem was due to war losses. This view persisted long after it should have been discarded and thus militated against the growth of confidence.

The notion is still prevalent though sometimes expressed rather differently. A specific case may be cited not merely by way of rebuttal but in order to clarify the issue further.

In a recent work[1] Harrod adopts a similar approach. 'The financial losses overseas, whether by the destruction or sale of capital assets or by the incurring of liabilities has been the central feature of the British post-war problem. . . . The British balance of payments problem has been particularly acute owing to the wartime losses . . .' The assertion is supported by pointing out that while before the war invisible receipts paid for one-third of United Kingdom imports, the comparable figure for 1960 was only 1·5 per cent. Reference is made to investment income, the loss of shipping receipts and Government overseas expenditure.

As a preliminary objection it seems unjustifiable to take data for 1960 as evidence of wartime losses: a year in the later 1940s would be more appropriate. In the interim there had been large fluctuations: although net invisibles in 1960 hardly exceeded £100 million, the total had been as high as £450 million in 1952.

A full statement would also reject the reference to the loss of shipping receipts: for years after the war these were much greater than before the war. Similarly, reference to the sale of overseas investments omits the fact that gross investment income in 1960 was three times as large as in 1938 while by this time the sterling balances created during the war had been repaid (see pp. 80–2). In so far as the invisible debits represented Government expenditure it should have been

[1] R. F. Harrod: *The British Economy* (McGraw-Hill, 1963), pp. 10, 12–13.

noted that this had been substantially reduced soon after the war but increased fivefold between 1952 and 1960, partly due to the incidence of Aid.

After making these points it still remains true that net invisibles at twice the pre-war figure (as in 1952) covered a much smaller proportion of imports than formerly. The operative factor, however, was not a reduction for invisible receipts (expressed in money terms) but the increase in price levels: world prices were now two to three times higher than before the war.

Even without war losses, higher prices would have impaired the current balance: as the United Kingdom had a pre-war import surplus of £300 million, a twofold rise in price levels would have raised the visible deficit to £600 million if export and import volume remained as before. Under the most favourable conditions not all the invisible credits could have risen to an equivalent extent: a country like the United Kingdom with income from abroad largely derived from fixed-interest investments would be adversely affected to a special degree. Other invisible credits respond more readily to price changes but being (as they were) relatively small, could meet the increased deficit only in part.

When the problem created by higher price levels is stated, emphasis on the trade deficit becomes more intelligible. Thus, although the White Paper analysis based on war losses was faulty, the policy proposed for the current balance seemed reasonable: a massive expansion of exports was declared as the primary objective. It was estimated that allowing for war losses a 50 per cent increase in export volume would pay for pre-war imports and show a surplus but the export target was set at a 75 per cent increase in order to realise a surplus which would permit of some increase in imports and the repayment of debt.

Two points arise in connection with the policy of export expansion. Initially, it was open to doubt whether the policy was realistic: would the objective be attained? A more searching critique would ask whether the attainment of the objective would solve the balance of payments problem.

There was some reason to think that the target figure proposed in the White Paper was too ambitious. It is relatively easy to secure a large increase in exports from a country where they have hitherto been negligible or where they account for only a minor part of the country's total trade. Such conditions were inapplicable to the United Kingdom: the export trade already bulked large in the economy and the country before the war had been the world's main exporter of manufactures. Under such circumstances the attempt to expand the volume of exports by 75 per cent seemed unlikely to succeed. Moreover, the target had to be considered in relation to the secular trend, which was highly adverse: between 1913 and 1938 export volume had fallen by over 40 per cent. Thus if the objective was to be attained it was necessary not merely to recover ground lost as a result of the war but also to reverse the trend which had developed in the preceding quarter-century. The prospects of success were the more doubtful in that the United States had been able to increase its share of world trade during the war while the progress of industrialisation in under-developed countries could be regarded as an additional obstacle.

Despite these obstacles the objective laid down was in fact quickly secured and there was not, as had been feared, any relapse after the initial expansion. Index numbers for export and import volume are given in the following table:

VOLUME OF TRADE

(1958 = 100)

	Exports	Imports
1913	91	81
1938	52	92
1946	52	62
1950	91	78
1958	100	100

Source: *London and Cambridge Economic Bulletin.*

For present purposes it is unnecessary to ask how the objective was attained. The expansion of world trade facilitated progress but for years after the war it was considered essential to retain direct controls on export production (motor vehicles, one of the main export groups, were not freely available on the home market until the 1950s). In the balance of trade context it is however material that despite the high import content of United Kingdom exports, there was no embarrassing increase in imports: it was not until 1955, when export volume had risen nearly twofold, that import volume regained the pre-war level. Here again direct controls were freely used: food rationing, for example, was maintained into the early 1950s and there were controls for many unrationed items.

Nevertheless, the export drive did not, as had been hoped, solve the balance of payments problem. Despite the satisfactory trend for exports (and for imports, too) there were crises in 1947 and 1949; the reserves, considered inadequate at the end of the war, had by 1949 fallen heavily and it was thought necessary to devalue sterling. Thus, although the target figure had been reached, the basic policy of restoring the balance of payments through an expansion of exports had failed.

In assigning reasons for this failure it cannot be said that the target figure was fixed too low. The estimate of 75 per cent increase in export volume had been computed on the assumption that invisible receipts would be much smaller than before the war: as in fact invisibles soon recovered to above the pre-war level the target figure was excessive. Nor did the growth of exports cease when the target had been attained: a further expansion was recorded during the 1950s and before the end of the decade the volume of exports was approximately twice as great as before the war.

The effect on the trade balance has already been demonstrated: the traditional gap between exports and imports was closed. Yet even this was insufficient. The record for the first post-war quinquennium and for the 1950s as well clearly implied that the problem could not be solved through a massive increase in exports: the target figure had been reached (and indeed exceeded) but the problem remained.

The persistence of the problem is sometimes taken as evidence that United Kingdom export performance has been poor. But such a judgment is superficial in that it omits several relevant factors and ambiguous because different standards can be used to assess results.

First, export performance may be compared with some earlier level of exports. On this criterion the United Kingdom record must be accounted outstandingly good: over a relatively brief period a twofold increase in export volume is a notable achievement for a country with an economy already geared to an unusually large export trade.

Alternatively, a comparison may be made with the record for other countries. Here the results seem less impressive as the United Kingdom share of world trade in manufactures declined during the 1950s and by the end of the decade was appreciably smaller than before the war. On the other hand, a declining trend has been evident for about a hundred years and it would be rash to conclude that export performance has been continuously poor when there was simultaneously a massive increase in export volume (which is the operative factor for the balance of payments).

Yet another measure of export performance is capacity to earn sufficient to balance outgoings. On this basis, too, the record is good: for visible trade alone the increase as compared with pre-war is under 50 per cent for import volume with export volume over 100 per cent. Moreover, despite large new debits in the current balance, the United Kingdom has been able to pay its way. The argument here is not affected by the recurrence of short-lived crises since solvency is properly taken as the cumulative total over a period.

On any or all of these criteria it would be unreasonable to fault export performance. But post-war experience implies that an expansion of exports is not enough to ensure solvency and in retrospect the defects of such a policy are apparent. Even for a limited objective such as equilibrium in the current account, export promotion may fail: the degree of expansion required to attain the objective will be uncertain, especially if the debits are constantly increasing: under such circumstances *any* increase in exports may be nullified (in whole or in part) by the invisibles (as during the 1950s).

When the objective is not merely equilibrium in the current balance but also an increase in the reserves, the creation of a current surplus is largely irrelevant: the United Kingdom normally earns a surplus only with the overseas sterling area and this does not yield international (i.e. non-sterling) currency. The reserves themselves, moreover, may be adversely affected by other factors such as reactions from the overseas sterling area or the impact of capital outflows. Such factors can easily offset a current surplus induced by rising exports.

Failure to accept these factors as elements in the sterling problem must hinder the formulation of a fully-articulated policy. Yet some at least were not only operative but evident during the early post-war years and will be examined in due course.

ii. THE DOLLAR SHORTAGE AND DEVALUATION

The diagnosis considered in the preceding section has now to be discarded in favour of an alternative based on the dollar problem as it arose after the war. In the context of this problem the White Paper analysis was defective on at least two counts. First, it was limited to the United Kingdom balance of payments and thus did not cover the sterling area as a whole: in particular the role of overseas sterling countries in relation to the central reserves was omitted. Secondly, it did not allow for the prospect of a dollar shortage which would adversely affect international payments.

The omissions were possibly deliberate. Given the occasion for which the White Paper was prepared (as set out in its title) and United States dislike of the sterling area, it may have seemed advisable to avoid emphasis on the system even at the cost of presenting an unrealistic picture. Not less important, perhaps, was the fact that Keynes, who was then influential in policy-making, had reached the conclusion that dollar shortage was an unlikely contingency.[1]

After a few years a more realistic analysis was evolved on the basis of experience. Before the end of the 1940s it had become clear that the dollar problem was in fact a major issue: in consequence the vital role of the overseas sterling area was now appreciated.

Both these points were explicitly mentioned in the official announcement of the decision to devalue sterling in 1949. As Parliament was in recess this announcement took the form of a broadcast by the Chancellor of the Exchequer which described

'. . . the difficulty that we and all the other non-dollar nations have in earning enough dollars to buy what we need in the way of food and raw materials, especially from America and Canada. It is referred to as the dollar shortage, or the sterling–dollar problem . . . it has become much more intense since the last war and indeed in the last few months our dollar difficulty in the sterling area has become very, very serious indeed. . . . We and the sterling countries of the Commonwealth like Australia and India and so on all do a lot of business with the dollar area and we pool our dollar earnings. So, though this problem affects the United Kingdom particularly — as bankers for the sterling area — it also affects the whole sterling area. . . .'

The Chancellor noted the progress of post-war recovery, pointing out that production was at a record level, exports half as much again as before the war, and the current balance in equilibrium. Nevertheless, it had not proved possible to earn enough dollars to meet current needs and latterly a failure of confidence had caused a drain on the reserves. The capital outflow was one reason for the decision to devalue; the other reason was the need to earn more dollars and thus effect a permanent solution for the dollar problem.

This statement represents a more comprehensive appraisal

[1] Lord Keynes: *The Balance of Payments of the United States* (Economic Journal, June 1946).

than that given in the White Paper issued at the end of the war. The approach based on war losses is by implication superseded; the reality of the dollar problem is appreciated and the role of the sterling area is recognised; allowance is made for capital movements as well as for the current balance. Since the statement was addressed to a popular audience it was naturally phrased in rather loose terms and the issues must now be defined more closely.[1]

The dollar problem was not peculiar to the United Kingdom and the other members of the sterling area: after the war most countries found it necessary to conserve dollars as far as possible in order to balance outgoings against receipts and even with restrictions on dollar imports it did not always prove easy to secure a balance. The sterling area as a whole was involved in the problem because member countries contributed to the central reserves and drew on the pool for dollar supplies.

The incidence of the problem is evident in the figures for the dollar trade of sterling countries shown overleaf.

It will be seen from the table that on both sides of the account there had been a large expansion as compared with pre-war, with no great disparity between exports and imports: by 1948 the dollar exports of the whole sterling area had risen almost threefold (in value terms) with very nearly the same increase for imports. The detail makes clear the new predominance of the overseas sterling area in relation to the United Kingdom: imports into the latter rose by about 600 million dollars while in the former (hitherto much the smaller sector) the increase was more than twice as great. This trend marked the emergence of the post-war dollar problem.

Part of the deficit was due to higher world prices but volume changes were also significant. Even after the exceptional totals for 1947 had been reduced by agreed measures to restrict imports, the impact from the overseas sterling area was apparent. The problem was eased by the reduction of

[1] For a more detailed exposition than is given here reference may be made to A. R. Conan: *The Sterling Area* (Macmillan, 1952).

imports into the United Kingdom: the 1948 volume index shows a figure 30 per cent *below* pre-war. In the overseas sterling area, however, there was a twofold *increase* for import volume.

DOLLAR TRADE OF THE STERLING AREA
(*US dollars million*)

	Pre-war*	1948
United Kingdom:		
Exports	300	700
Imports	800	1400
Balance	−500	−700
Rest of Sterling Area:		
Exports	400	1200
Imports	350	1600
Balance	50	−400
All Sterling Area:		
Trade Balance	−450	−1100
Gold Output	500	500

VOLUME OF DOLLAR TRADE
(1938 = 100)

United Kingdom:		
Exports	100	130
Imports	100	70
Rest of Sterling Area:		
Exports	100	201
Imports	100	199
All Sterling Area:		
Exports	100	171
Imports	100	110

* Average, 1934–38.

Source: Trade figures from United States and Canadian official returns (covering trade with these two countries only). Index numbers from ECE: *Economic Bulletin for Europe*, October 1949.

The net effect on the trade balance can be summarised as follows. The overseas sterling area now had a substantial deficit (400 million dollars) in lieu of the former surplus; heavier imports thus involved a deterioration of 450 million dollars for this sector. The United Kingdom balance also deteriorated (by 200 million dollars) despite larger exports and a reduction in import volume: here the adverse trend was solely due to higher prices.

For the sterling system as a whole the result was a heavy increase in the import surplus (from 500 million to 1100 million dollars). It was impracticable to cover the gap in the same way as formerly because the gold output of sterling countries (500 million dollars) was no greater than before the war.

With the central reserve system in operation the data reveal the origins of the sterling–dollar problem in the early post-war years: it arose for the most part outside the United Kingdom. Recapitulation of the main points will demonstrate the dominant role of the overseas sector.

First, there was a large increase in the sterling area's adverse balance for dollar trade although in volume terms the United Kingdom was exporting more and importing less.

Secondly, the overseas sterling area showed a deficit instead of a surplus on dollar trade account.

Thirdly, as the dollar price of gold was unchanged, the gold output (formerly much the largest dollar-earner) now purchased in real terms only half as much as before the war.

None of these three factors can be traced to a failure in the United Kingdom economy although London as banker for the system registered the impact. It may be said that even if the deficit originated elsewhere, the United Kingdom ought to have found an appropriate remedy: this, however, is merely to say that there was an obligation (what sort of obligation?) to solve the dollar problems of other countries as well as its own.

In fact the United Kingdom had solved its balance of payments problem as stated at the end of the war: by 1948 there was a surplus on current account. It had also contributed to the solution of the sterling area's dollar problem by increasing dollar exports and reducing dollar imports. Criticism of the failure to secure an exact balance of dollar receipts against dollar payments is inadmissible. To assert that the United Kingdom ought to have attained such a balance assumes a crude form of bilateralism: no advocate of multilateral trade can claim that the existence of a *dollar* deficit signifies a failure in balance of payments policy.

Yet that deficit was of special concern to the custodian of the central reserves and remedial action of some kind seemed essential. The choice of an appropriate policy was, however, limited by circumstances. So far as the United Kingdom was concerned, it was doubtful whether an established pattern of trade and payments could be readily modified to balance dollar outgoings against receipts (though a further improvement could not be ruled out). Again, the fact that disequilibrium in the dollar account had originated overseas meant that there might be only limited scope for United Kingdom policy unless it was supported by similar policies for the overseas sector. Under such conditions the point at issue was whether the devaluation of the pound as against the dollar could be justified.

The official announcement of the decision to devalue stated two main objectives. The first aim was to stem the capital outflow. Once the prospect of a new rate seemed imminent, the forces making for a continued outflow probably became irresistible and could only be met by devaluation. The adoption of such a policy, however, would not by itself ensure a complete cessation of capital exports. It was still necessary to maintain controls on the movement of funds to non-sterling countries and there were later instances (e.g. in 1957) when these movements occasioned severe strain. Thus the new policy was in this respect not fully effective.

Devaluation as a measure intended to right the current balance of the United Kingdom with the dollar area was much less urgent. The case for action here was not conclusive, since no gross disequilibrium was apparent. In 1948 a deficit of some £250 million (swollen by imports under ERP programmes) was covered to the extent of nearly £150 million by ERP grants; the net deficit (after taking credit for these grants) was only £100 million while the shortfall for the first half of 1949 was 20 per cent less than a year earlier. A dollar deficit of that magnitude does not appear unmanageable: although import controls were still needed, dollar imports were at the time unusually large because other sources of supply were not freely accessible.

This seems to have been the official view: the repeated denials of the intention to devalue suggest that the authorities were not convinced of the need for such a step.

There was other evidence to confirm such a view. Dollar exports were rising at a satisfactory rate: an increase of 30 per cent in volume over pre-war as early as 1948 hardly implied any lack of competitiveness and data for the cost and price structure do not support the notion that devaluation was imperative in order to stimulate exports even further. Allowing for the 1939 devaluation of sterling, the indexes for wages and prices had risen less (in the case of wages very much less) than the corresponding indexes for the United States while the trend for export prices in the two countries was similar. On such evidence it could not be maintained that the dollar trade balance had lapsed into disequilibrium which could only be corrected by devaluation.[1]

The conclusion corroborates the view that the real trouble lay elsewhere. With the overseas sterling area in deficit to an extent which absorbed nearly all the current gold output, there was a case for action in that sector if the mechanism were to function smoothly.

It is not quite so clear that devaluation was the appropriate remedy, especially as this policy could not be imposed on the rest of the sterling area. The decision to devalue affected only the exchange value of the pound for the United Kingdom and the Colonies: other members of the system could keep the existing rate with sterling and thus devalue as against the dollar or keep the existing rate with the dollar and appreciate as against sterling (or adopt an intermediate course). Not all of them wished to follow sterling but in the end all except Pakistan decided to do so.

The character of the sterling system makes it hard to say

[1] See table on p. 27 of Harrod: *The Pound Sterling* (Princeton Essays in International Finance, 1952).

whether this decision was calculated to right the dollar balance of the overseas sector: such a large group of countries cannot properly be treated as a unified economy since its members differed greatly in economic structure while in the special context of the dollar problem their needs were diverse. In any case the decision to devalue was generally based not on the state of the dollar balance but on the prospective loss which would be involved in appreciation of their currencies against sterling.

If, however, it were safe to generalise for the overseas sterling area as a whole, an appraisal would suggest certain defects in the policy adopted.

One weakness in this policy was its limited value as a stimulus to exports. The impact would hardly be the same as in the United Kingdom, since devaluation would concern primarily raw materials and foodstuffs rather than manufactures. These commodities normally sell at prices which reflect a complex of market forces in addition to production costs: this aspect was soon afterwards demonstrated by the outbreak of the Korean war. Moreover, the quantities which can be sold at any time are more dependent on factors such as the state of industrial activity or stock-piling than on current prices. Devaluation, therefore, would not necessarily lower the dollar price of sterling area commodities or bring any great increase in sales. In fact the deficit disappeared when the dollar prices of sterling commodities *rose* sharply during the Korea boom.

Another weakness was that devaluation did not directly affect the returns from gold (the largest dollar-earner) since the dollar price of gold remained as before. Thus in so far as the deficit of the overseas sterling area was attributable to the reduction in the purchasing power of gold, the new policy had no immediate impact. (There were, however, indirect effects since the increase in the sterling price of gold acted as a stimulus to output.)

Perhaps the primary objective was a reduction in the overseas sterling area's dollar imports. Although these were already restricted by direct controls, higher prices for dollar goods (after a 30 per cent devaluation) would probably be a more effective means of saving dollars, as for various reasons the controls were not always easy to enforce. Such a differential compared with sterling goods would facilitate a switch to sterling sources of supply and if dollar imports were reduced, it would be reasonable to expect also some reduction in the deficit for invisibles such as shipping costs, etc.

The immediate impact of devaluation can be traced only up to June 1950 since thereafter the trend was affected by the outbreak of war in Korea and the associated commodity boom. Within this brief period, however, the sterling area's dollar account was transformed. The trade balance responded rapidly: in the last quarter of 1949 the deficit was the smallest of the year while in 1950, as the United Kingdom deficit fell and the surplus of other sterling countries rose, a favourable trade balance emerged (in the second quarter) for the sterling area as a whole. This, however, was due much more to the restriction of imports than to the expansion of exports: for January–June 1950 exports were only 100 million dollars greater than a year earlier but the reduction in imports was about 600 million dollars.

Thus, despite the quick response from the trade balance, there was at the outset little to show that devaluation would stimulate exports while as regards imports it is impracticable to distinguish the effect of devaluation from the effect of the decision to reduce dollar expenditure by 25 per cent.

The longer-term trend for dollar trade is not now a matter for speculation as data are available over an extended period. The trend for the 1950s shown in the table (p. 44) is clear in outline but not easy to interpret. On the export side there is a marked contrast between the United Kingdom and the overseas sterling area: in the former case exports were almost doubled between 1950 and 1956 while in the latter case there was no substantial change, the total being under £500 million at both dates. If, therefore, devaluation was intended to stimulate the dollar earnings of overseas sterling countries, it failed to do so.

DOLLAR TRADE OF THE STERLING AREA

£ million

	United Kingdom			Rest of Sterling Area		
	Exports	Imports	Balance	Exports	Imports	Balance
1950	323	439	−116	465	350	115
1951	392	742	−350	632	602	30
1952	408	606	−198	464	605	−141
1953	441	517	−76	412	432	−20
1954	420	556	−136	403	440	−37
1955	494	731	−237	478	515	−37
1956	620	769	−149	478	572	−94
1957	636	826	−190	543	684	−141

Source: *United Kingdom Balance of Payments, 1946–57* (HMSO, 1959).

The contrast between the two sectors during these years exemplifies the risks of generalisation on so diversified an economy as the sterling area. The inability of the overseas sector to expand its earnings has to be set against the enormous increase recorded for the United Kingdom (following a 75 per cent expansion in the volume of total exports attained earlier). On one view the increase would register the effect of devaluation although such a view would perhaps be opposed by those who hold that devaluation accentuated inflationary pressure in the economy: furthermore, the competitive advantage expected from devaluation was largely offset by the devaluation of other currencies. Alternatively, the increase between 1952 and 1956 could be taken as a response to the deflationary policies initiated by raising Bank rate in 1951: this conclusion, however, hardly accords with the view that the persistence of chronic inflation throughout the 1950s was responsible for 'unsatisfactory' export performance. Perhaps a valid conclusion is that the United Kingdom's dollar exports proved fully competitive: thus the data must again tell against the theory that chronic inflation acted as a drag on exports.

The trend for imports is equally hard to evaluate because of the multiple factors involved. Direct controls on dollar trade were retained by the United Kingdom and the overseas sterling area; the devaluation of sterling was an additional restrictive factor: inflationary pressure (if it existed) would work in the opposite direction and so (perhaps) would imports of capital from the United States. Moreover, direct controls were relaxed or extended as required while inflationary pressure was probably also variable. The effect of devaluation, therefore, cannot be isolated.

For the United Kingdom at least the impact was slight if only because dollar imports were already tightly controlled: the total in 1949 was in real terms less, and in 1950 very much less, than before the war. Thus there was relatively little scope for further restriction especially as about 75 per cent of the total comprised food, feedingstuffs and raw materials which were not then readily available from non-dollar sources. This did not apply to the overseas sterling area where dollar imports were mainly manufactured goods which could also be supplied from the United Kingdom.

The data in fact do not register any marked restriction of dollar imports after an initial reduction in 1951 which may have been the result of direct controls. As late as 1953–56 imports into both the United Kingdom and the rest of the sterling area were probably in real terms about the same as in 1948–49 and for the two preceding years had been higher.

In general the conclusion must be that devaluation did not solve the problem of dollar trade. The United Kingdom still had a deficit while the overseas sterling area reverted to deficit after the boom of 1950–51 (which cannot be attributed to devaluation). As a result, the dollar trade balance of the whole sterling area was continuously adverse after the Korea boom and in the later 1950s this deficit involved a heavy drain on the central reserves.

The failure of even a large adjustment to redress the dollar balance hardly recommends devaluation as an instrument of policy but since in recent years further use of the instrument has been advocated the policy may be reconsidered not merely in the context of the dollar problem (now quiescent) but in relation to the United Kingdom's balance as a whole.

A preliminary point should be explicitly stated: in 1949

the United Kingdom did not effect an all-round devaluation of sterling in terms of other currencies. The pound was devalued in terms of the dollar but as the overseas sterling area and most other non-dollar countries acted likewise, the end-result for the United Kingdom was a partial devaluation: its extent may be gauged from the fact that in 1949 dollar exports comprised hardly more than 10 per cent of the total. As there was no alteration in exchange rates with the overseas sterling area (which accounted for about one-half of the United Kingdom's external trade) or with most non-sterling non-dollar countries, the devaluation did not directly affect the United Kingdom's trade and payments as a whole although there may have been indirect effects (dollar goods being now relatively expensive for the non-dollar world). Thus with devaluation fully operative only over a narrow sector, its impact was limited.

The point is relevant to the debate on another possible devaluation. In the context of the dollar problem it was no doubt appropriate that the adjustment deemed necessary should be limited to the dollar trade sector: the case is different when devaluation is advocated to reinforce the current balance as a whole.

The Radcliffe Committee discussed the conditions which would justify such a step. It distinguished between two sets of circumstances. The first related to a situation where there was a progressive deterioration in the competitive position of United Kingdom exports on world markets:

In such a situation the relevant consideration is the movement in the price of United Kingdom exports, mainly manufactures, compared with the price of similar goods manufactured elsewhere. Devaluation, which might seem capable of restoring the position, could accomplish little in the short run because it takes a good deal of time and considerable outlay in selling costs for most types of manufactures to win their way in export markets, especially those markets in which sales effort has not previously been concentrated. But if the competitive handicap has been persistent and the devaluation more than removes it, the price advantage that results should not only bring to an end the gradual loss of markets but should eventually reverse the process.[1]

The second situation was described by the Committee in the following terms:

Competitive power must be measured, not against some previous level of comparative costs, but in relation to the structural adjustments in exports and imports that have to be accomplished. If exports are insufficient to yield a satisfactory balance of payments, or if overseas demand falls off for the range of goods in which the British export trades specialise, it may be necessary to accept a lower price in order to secure the necessary increase in earnings. Any attempt on the United Kingdom's part to obtain a larger share of world trade in manufactures must involve the offer either of a more attractive range of exports . . . or of the traditional range of exports on more attractive terms. Devaluation can make the terms on which British goods are offered more attractive and, if the response of foreign customers is elastic, will add to export earnings. Thus it is a measure which may have to be taken if long-term changes in the structure of world markets or in the relationship between the components of the United Kingdom's balance of payments are throwing the economy progressively out of external balance.[2]

In both cases the Committee considered that it would be preferable to deal with the difficulty by methods (unspecified) other than devaluation: only if these proved ineffective would it be right to consider an alteration in the exchange rate. It thus envisaged devaluation not as a normal instrument of monetary policy but as

a measure capable, in default of acceptable alternatives, of bringing about some enduring adjustment in the country's economic structure, correcting some long-standing lack of balance in its competitive position, or checking any violent . . . deflationary pressure that may reach it from abroad.[3]

[1] *Report*, para 715. [2] Ibid., para 717. [3] Ibid., para 718.

The Committee did not apply its analysis to the 1949 situation nor did it assess the impact of devaluation at that time. On the evidence summarised earlier it could hardly be said that in 1949 United Kingdom exports were becoming progressively non-competitive but conditions then were in one sense not unlike the second situation envisaged by the Committee, since it could be held that the dollar problem called for structural adjustments in order to improve the current balance. In the early 1960s, although the dollar problem had disappeared, a somewhat similar view was put forward and its advocates began to press for another devaluation.

This new proposal postulated that the growth of the United Kingdom economy was inadequate (relative to other countries, especially in Europe) and that the attainment of a higher growth rate was dependent on a large increase in exports: assuming that the competitive power of the United Kingdom in world trade was declining, such an increase could be secured only by devaluation.

It was not altogether clear whether the proposal involved a devaluation of the pound in relation to other currencies generally or merely in relation to the dollar: if the latter, it would again constitute only a partial devaluation (with a limited effect on the export trade as a whole) and as the dollar shortage had ended such a step would be less defensible than in 1949. Nor was it clear why the earlier experiment (which had failed to solve the sterling problem) should be repeated, unless on the ground that devaluation was needed every ten or twelve years to keep in step with the rest of the world.[1]

In fact there seemed to be very little direct evidence that a further alteration was necessary. Those who held that the effects of the 1949 devaluation had been exhausted by the continued rise in wages and export prices omitted to note the existence of similar trends elsewhere. During the 1950s wage costs rose much more in Europe than in the United

[1] In 1949 the change in the rate had been made unusually large in order to avoid another in the foreseeable future.

Kingdom: by the end of the decade hourly earnings (including social charges) for manufacturing industry were no higher than in Germany and only one-third of those in the United States.[1] The favourable trend continued into the 1960s: a study of comparative costs for 1961 showed that with the United States rated at 100, the United Kingdom would stand at 84 and the European Economic Community at 96.[2] Such data afford no support to the view that the pound was over-valued at the existing exchange rate and might imply the contrary.[3]

Further data could be cited to the same effect. In this context steel is of basic significance for industrial countries and may fairly be taken as representative of the general trend. After nearly twenty years of post-war inflation (with allegedly inferior technology and supposedly low productivity) United Kingdom steel prices in 1965 were by a considerable margin lower than domestic prices in either Western Europe or the United States.[4] The United Kingdom was thus able to capture markets in Europe during the early 1960s while steel sales to the United States rose from £9 million in 1961 to an annual rate of £25 million in the first half of 1965.

If, however, there was little direct evidence for over-valuation of the pound, there was some indirect evidence which could be interpreted to show that exports were lagging. Between 1954 and 1962 the United Kingdom share of world trade in manufactures had declined from 20 per cent to 15 per cent. This trend might mean that

[1] See the table quoted in Wells: *British Export Performance* (Cambridge University Press, 1964), p. 83. Also the data in MacDougall: *The Dollar Problem, A Reappraisal* (*Princeton Essays in International Finance*, 1960), p. 22.

[2] Report of the National Industrial Conference Board of the United States, quoted in *Statist*, 8 December 1961.

[3] Hawtrey has consistently maintained the view that sterling has been under-valued since 1949. Cf. *The Balance of Payments and the Standard of Living* (Royal Institute of International Affairs, 1950), p. 101; *Is Sterling Under-Valued?* (*Financial Times*, 13 January 1958).

[4] Comparative statement issued by Iron and Steel Board and published in *Financial Times*, 12 April 1965.

exports had become non-competitive for price or other reasons.

The conclusion seems unwarranted. As the United Kingdom share of world trade has been declining since 1870, the argument implies that for almost a century British exports have been non-competitive (which is possibly true in a narrowly formal sense) and the pound over-valued (which is much more disputable): it takes no account of special factors operative in the 1950s such as the incidence of Aid Programmes, the end of dollar discrimination, and the creation of new preferences in Europe. Moreover, between 1954 and 1962 the United States share of world trade declined to about the same extent as the British share: on this evidence American exports also must be accounted non-competitive and a case could be made for the devaluation of the dollar. With the United States in the early 1960s running an export surplus of some 5 billion dollars per annum, the argument would not perhaps be very convincing.

The case against United Kingdom exports is further weakened by evidence that they were fully competitive in markets where they received no preferences and were often without the benefit of established connections. Between 1955 and 1960 sales to the United States and Europe rose by 97 per cent and 30 per cent, respectively: the obstacles to expansion were encountered not in these highly competitive markets but in the so-called protected markets of the Commonwealth or the overseas sterling area.

It was even doubtful whether the decline in the United Kingdom share of world trade could be linked with the trend for productivity. There was evidence that productivity in the United Kingdom had been rising more slowly than in several other countries, with adverse effects on wage costs, but the National Economic Development Council in a critical survey of export trends[1] could find no close connection between wage costs and export performance. Although in the United Kingdom a substantial increase in costs per unit of output coincided with a marked decline in

[1] NEDC: *Export Trends* (HMSO, 1963), para 40.

the country's share of world exports, a similar increase in the Netherlands did not produce a like effect (the Dutch share of world exports rose slightly): again, Germany was able to increase its share of world trade despite a sharp rise in unit costs while the reverse was true for the United States where costs were nearly stable. With such diverse experience it was far from certain that an attempt to lower costs via the exchange rate would automatically improve export performance.

On the whole, therefore, the case for further devaluation of the pound was shaky. For several reasons it was also doubtful whether such a policy, if adopted, would be effective.

Apart from the failure of the 1949 devaluation to solve (as was intended) the balance of payments problem, the issues were now more complex. If in fact (as suggested above) exports were not hampered by an over-valued pound, there was limited scope for an improvement even in the trade balance; if (as will be suggested in the next section) there was little evidence of inflationary pressure attracting imports, devaluation would not only be unnecessary but actually harmful in that it would increase the cost of essential imports such as food and raw materials. Nor can the proposal be discussed in terms of visible trade alone since the new balance of payments structure enters into the problem. On a broader view devaluation would involve (as formerly it had not) a heavier burden for two of the main debits, investment payments and Government expenditure. The total impact on the investment income account might well be favourable (since there is a net credit for the category as a whole) if the pound were devalued against other currencies generally (i.e. not merely as against the dollar) but this would not be true of the Government account, where there is a large net debit. Any proposal for devaluation should therefore assess its impact on the diverse components of the current balance.

In retrospect, the two occasions since the war when devaluation became a matter of practical policy can be seen

to have differed in character. On the earlier occasion, in 1949, the dollar shortage constituted the immediate problem and devaluation as a policy was explicitly related to this problem, not to any failure of the current balance. On the next occasion, in the early 1960s, the dollar problem had receded but devaluation was advocated as a measure to reinforce the current account.

In each case a realistic study must raise doubts as to whether devaluation was appropriate. The data were inconclusive while on the evidence available in 1949 and again in the 1960s it was possible to make a case for the devaluation of the dollar as well as (or instead of) the pound; in neither case, moreover, was there convincing evidence of persistent disequilibrium in the current balance. Such conditions underline the limitations of analysis in the field of exchange-rate policy.

A policy appraisal should also note the results (so far as they are ascertainable) of the 1949 devaluation. The data presented here suggest that the new rate was ineffective as a solution for the sterling–dollar problem: the adoption of another policy in the early 1950s implies that it was similarly ineffective for the sterling problem as a whole.

So far the review has shown that two major policies had been tried and had proved of doubtful value: a third attempt to diagnose and solve the problem must now be considered.

iii. INFLATION AND DEFLATION

The doctrine which linked the problem of sterling to the dollar problem continued to receive support during the 1950s though perhaps with diminishing emphasis: towards the end of the decade it was discarded, not because devaluation had proved effective but because the dollar shortage itself ended. Meanwhile, there was fairly general acceptance of the doctrine that the emergence or persistence of the sterling problem was due to inflation.

The diagnosis was not new. Some economists had maintained that the crisis of 1947 was a result of inflation; others attributed the 1949 devaluation to the same cause; a third crisis, in 1951, showed the need for a theory which would account for these recurrent strains. In view of the favourable balance of payments trend up to 1950 it was increasingly unrealistic to state the problem in terms of war losses; it was also less plausible to explain it by reference to the dollar shortage or an over-valued pound since such obstacles should have been eliminated by devaluation. As, however, the third post-war crisis seemed to imply that the problem had not yet been solved, a definitive analysis was required.

This was provided in an authoritative version by Robbins at the end of 1951; ten years later the same doctrine dictated the measures adopted to meet the crisis of 1961. During the intervening period it was variously stated. In the Robbins version[1] the operative factor was not defined with precision but loosely designated 'inflationary pressure'; later, economists distinguished between 'cost inflation' and 'demand inflation'; later still it was assumed that inflation (in some sense) or 'over-heating of the economy' was attributable to the process of growth.

On a broad view the doctrine as usually stated hardly fits the facts. The inflation analysis is primarily relevant to visible trade and takes little account of the invisible items which now bulk so large in the total; it is thus unrealistic in positing an over-simplified balance of payments model. Again, the inflation theory is normally applied to the United Kingdom alone and neglects the role of the overseas sterling area as a determinant of the reserves. Finally, inflation can explain only a deterioration in the current balance (apart from secondary effects on confidence) while in nearly all crises since the war capital flows have been prominent.

It is therefore advisable to ask for rather strict proofs when inflation is put forward as the supposed cause of post-war difficulties. In fact the proofs are rarely forthcoming. Sometimes it is considered sufficient to note signs of inflation and claim that balance of payments weakness must inevitably

[1] Robbins: *The Balance of Payments.*

follow, although of course inflation *per se* does not necessarily harm even the trade balance: an adverse effect can appear only when inflation proceeds at a more rapid rate than elsewhere. Furthermore, while it is never easy to find comparable data for different countries which will serve to measure changes in relative costs and prices, it is seldom possible to secure agreement on the interpretation of the data.

These points can be illustrated from the studies by Robbins and Harrod to which reference has already been made. Robbins, in a statement which relies heavily on the classical theory of the trade balance, concedes that to some extent the originating cause of the post-war problem may have been external (i.e. war losses or, in 1949, a recession in the United States) but maintains that financial policy was at fault since it failed to offset such conditions. In that sense, at least, inflationary pressure is held responsible for the first three post-war crises (1947, 1949 and 1951) but the argument as summarised in the following passage seems to go much further, attributing to inflation a positive role as a disequilibrating factor:

> The inflationary pressure has not been sufficiently checked. In '46–47 there was the overt folly of the ultra-cheap money policy, which, together with some laxity as regards the export of capital, culminated in the crisis of '47. Then, for a time, a determined effort was made and our hopes began to revive. But, in the winter of '48–49, inflationary pressure again tended to become active: and the development of a very mild recession in the United States found us still so fundamentally weak that a major devaluation was necessary. Once more some initial effort was made to damp down the pressure; and in 1950 a most gratifying improvement took place. Then the coming of rearmament once more strengthened the incipient upward movement at home; and abroad it turned the terms of trade against us via the movement of raw material prices. A position existed, indeed, in which some positive curtailment of expenditure was desirable if external equilibrium was to be maintained.[1]

[1] Robbins, op. cit., pp. 19–20.

This type of diagnosis, presented with a minimum of factual evidence, is unacceptable. It interprets the 1947 crisis as mainly a failure of the current balance although the deficit was planned and covered while the United Kingdom dollar deficit (also covered) did not contribute to the drain on the reserves. It cannot explain the 1949 crisis (when the United Kingdom had a surplus on current account) except by noting the failure to attain a bilateral balance with the dollar area. It suggests that inflation in the United Kingdom during the early post-war years had been more intense than in the United States. Harrod, on the other hand, produces evidence for 1948–49 (already referred to on p. 41) which suggests the reverse: in his view the data for costs and prices imply that as between the dollar and the pound, devaluation of the former would have been more appropriate.[1]

On these grounds alone the diagnosis for both the 1947 and the 1949 crises must be rejected: it virtually ignores the drain on the dollar pool attributable to the overseas sterling area as well as the capital outflow. Moreover, in order to demonstrate a neat theory, the evidence is unjustifiably strained: thus recovery in 1948 as in 1950 is associated with the easing of inflationary pressure although in both cases other factors (including direct controls) were in operation. Again, no one would infer from the passage quoted that in 1950 (when there was 'a most gratifying improvement') the trade deficit was virtually the same as in 1949.

The 1951 crisis perhaps deserves special scrutiny. In that year (unlike 1947) the deficit was not foreseen but emerged suddenly and unexpectedly; unlike 1949 the current balance lapsed into heavy deficit, mainly on trade account. At the time, too, the economy could be regarded as susceptible to inflation since a massive rearmament programme started during the latter part of 1950: in addition, some economists held that the 1949 devaluation augmented inflationary pressures and these were certainly stimulated by imported inflation as a result of rising world commodity prices. On all counts, therefore, this case is crucial for testing the diagnosis.

[1] Harrod: *The Pound Sterling*, p. 27.

Yet inflationary pressure as generally understood was not primarily responsible. It is perhaps significant that on the export front the cumulative effect of the factors specified above seems to have been negligible. Export volume was no greater than in the preceding year but if this be taken as an adverse reaction it should be noted also that, despite the deflation initiated at the end of 1951, exports stagnated until 1955. The adverse trade balance was primarily due to imports, which were 50 per cent greater than a year earlier, with an increase of some 10 per cent in volume and import prices up by over 30 per cent.

Such data are inconsistent with the view that the 1951 deficit was occasioned by domestic inflation: external events were clearly responsible. The decision of Governments to rearm involved a sharp rise in commodity prices, primarily due to demand from the United States; the effect on the United Kingdom was accentuated because stocks had been run down when imports were restricted in 1950 (as heavier imports were in fact largely utilised for stock-building, the size of the deficit was misleading). In the main, therefore, the crisis was due to a political emergency (the Korea war) and the attempt to interpret the evidence as support for the inflation theory is unjustified.

One further case of a rapid deterioration may be briefly examined. In 1955 the current balance was again in deficit (although only to the extent of some £150 million). But the inflation diagnosis must here be regarded as suspect since the deterioration concerned the invisible items rather than visible trade: in the former category there was a reduction of nearly £200 million in net receipts while the adverse trade balance rose by hardly more than £100 million. Once again, inflationary pressure was not apparent in the export trend: the expansion in volume terms was much greater than in either 1953 or 1954. Failing adequate evidence the large increase in import volume cannot safely be ascribed to inflation but was more probably due to the relaxation of controls in 1954. This view seems corroborated by the fact that imports from sterling countries (which were mainly uncontrolled) rose by only 5 per cent while those from non-sterling sources rose by no less than 20 per cent. As in 1951, the increase in imports is misleading taken by itself since much of it went into stocks.

The history of post-war crises does not, therefore, confirm the theory that inflationary pressure was at the heart of the sterling problem and in certain cases implies the contrary. In both 1951 and 1955, for example, the mere fact that the deficit was a *sudden* rather than a gradual phenomenon (with, in each case, a surplus the year before and the year after) makes it probable that some other cause was at least partly responsible: erratic phenomena are unlikely to register variations in inflationary pressure since inflation or deflation cannot be regulated with an appropriate and immediate response from the balance of payments.

An alternative approach suggests that more significant than any crisis occasioned by special conditions in a particular year is the longer-term trend for the current balance. On this approach a very different picture emerges. The post-war recovery culminating in surpluses from 1948 to 1950 hardly indicates the presence of inflation. Similarly, the data for the 1950s as a whole rebut the notion that inflation was a continuous drag on the creation of a surplus.

The point becomes clearer when the results for this period are set out in detail. Disregarding year-to-year fluctuations, there was a steady improvement: the current surplus averaged £15 million for 1950–52, £60 million for 1954–56 and no less than £230 million for 1957–59 (each average covers good and bad years alike). The essential here is not the size of the balance but the trend: a constantly rising surplus is inconsistent with chronic inflation. It is scarcely a valid objection to say that until the end of the decade imports were restricted and the trade balance thus artificial: such an objection would be unjustified because similar conditions apply in all countries.

The conclusion implicit in the data is corroborated by the fact that the surplus comprised a deterioration for the invisible items and an improvement in the visible trade balance.

Net receipts from invisibles were as much as £450 million in 1952 but a few years later had fallen to little more than £100 million: this contrasts with a deficit of £400 million per annum for visible trade at the beginning of the decade (1950–51 average) and a virtual balance for exports and imports at its end (1956–59 average). Thus the elimination of the historic import surplus not only points to the absence of inflation but makes it clear that the absolute amount of the surplus on current account would have been much larger had it not been for the erosion of invisible receipts (which cannot be attributed to inflation).

It could of course be said that the generally favourable trend for the trade balance during the 1950s reflected the deflationary policy initiated by raising Bank rate in 1951. This policy and its results must now be summarised.

The background against which it should be viewed can be briefly outlined. By the end of 1951, with a huge deficit in the current balance, it seemed evident that a massive increase in exports had failed to maintain the balance in equilibrium; the devaluation of 1949 had likewise failed. There was thus a case for embarking on a new policy.

The increase of Bank rate to 4 per cent early in 1952 marked the definite adoption of deflation: this step was explicitly aimed at restoring the balance of payments and it was supported by other monetary measures (e.g. tighter controls on capital issues and bank advances) as well as by more severe restrictions on imports.

As noted on an earlier occasion, the effects of the various measures are not easy to distinguish: imports, for example, were restricted by direct controls as well as by deflation. But in so far as the new policy was intended to stimulate exports, it proved to be of dubious utility. The expansion of exports which was so notable a feature of the years 1946–50 (when inflation was said to be endemic) ceased: export volume in 1952–53 in fact averaged 5 per cent less than in 1950–51. On the other hand, although 1953–54 were years of deliberate reflation, the volume of exports rose quite considerably in 1954–55.

The experiment initiated by the use of monetary policy in the early 1950s thus gives little support to the claim that deflation can secure a quick response from the trade balance.

Ten years later the same policy was tried again: after another large deficit in 1960 a further dose of deflation was administered in 1961, this time assisted by a wage pause. Again the results were poor although conditions abroad were exceptionally favourable because the economy of Western Europe was in an inflationary phase. The response from exports was negligible: the rate of increase (in volume terms) for 1962 was less than in either of the two preceding years and only after reflation had started at the end of 1962 was there a marked upturn. There was, moreover, no sign that the renewed attempt at deflation had any effect in restraining the rise in export prices; over the whole period 1958–62 the average value of exports showed a steady increase at an annual rate which was virtually unchanged from year to year.

On the import side also the data do not suggest that the reaction was better in this second trial. The 1961 experiment is highly suitable as a test case since imports were now mostly free from direct controls. Although for that year the total was slightly less than in the preceding year, the reduction had become apparent before deflationary measures were introduced and in any event the 1962 total was appreciably above the abnormally large figure recorded two years earlier.

By the 1960s, therefore, there was evidence that the use of monetary policy to regulate the current balance was unsatisfactory: it was doubtfully effective in action and if it checked inflationary pressure, tended also to restrict the growth of the economy. The need was thus for a policy which should halt inflation without stunting growth.

The case for such a policy and the means by which it could be enforced were outlined in the Fourth Report of the Council on Prices, Productivity and Incomes: the Committee's recommendations were adopted by the Government in July 1961 and included among the measures taken to deal with the crisis of that year. As a short-term expedient a wage-pause was introduced 'in order to allow wages abroad to catch up with wages in the United Kingdom'. For the longer-term the new proposal was that over a specific period the increase in money incomes should not exceed the increase in productivity for that period. It was hoped to attain the objective through an incomes policy which would restrict any increase in wages and profits to a tolerable level.

As the proposal became a controversial issue some brief comments of a factual nature may be included here. Three points in particular are relevant.

First, the assumption that rising wages must push up export prices to an equivalent extent is unjustified. In 1960 wages were 7 per cent higher than in 1958 while export prices had risen by no more than 2 per cent; by 1964 the wage increase was as much as 30 per cent as against a price increase of only 9 per cent. Thus even a large increase in wages may have only a slight effect on the cost of exports.

It seems probable that the trend for output and productivity has a much greater effect. Between 1952 and 1955 there was an increase of over 20 per cent in hourly earnings but no considerable change in unit labour costs because during those years output and productivity were rising at virtually the same rate. On the other hand, between 1955 and 1958, when output and productivity were stagnating, an increase of 18 per cent in earnings brought an equivalent increase in costs.

No less relevant is the performance of the United Kingdom as compared with other countries. The official doctrine on the need for a wage policy assumes the existence of chronic inflation during the 1950s and the 1960s. In fact, after 'a decade of inflation' (so it was often termed) the United Kingdom was still competitive: as already seen (pp. 48–9) labour costs at the end of the 1950s were not out of line with those elsewhere, being no higher than in continental Europe as a whole and much less than in the United States. Subsequent events reinforced the position: between 1960 and 1963 wages in France and Germany rose by approximately

30 per cent (as compared with an increase of little more than 10 per cent for the United Kingdom) and as early as 1962 British wage costs (including social charges) were less than in either of the two former countries. With a reasonably favourable trend for productivity superimposed, wage costs per unit of output between 1961 and 1963 were stationary in the United Kingdom while in the Common Market countries they rose sharply and in the United States there was little change.[1]

The comparisons must weaken the view that an incomes policy is essential. If wages and export prices are only loosely related, such a policy would not ensure competitiveness just as high wages in the United States or Germany do not hamper exports from those countries. On the other hand there is nothing to show that the United Kingdom has become non-competitive because of unduly high wage-levels: for the 1960s at any rate the trend has been very much in its favour as compared with Europe.

Finally, the data taken with the balance of payments record illustrate the limitations of the proposed controls. The favourable trend for unit costs during recent years (perhaps more favourable than any likely to be secured through an incomes policy) did not prevent the development of a large import surplus in 1964: it may be inferred that the formal implementation of a policy for the control of costs cannot guarantee immunity from a deficit in the trade balance.

A more extended critique would revert to the initial diagnosis. The incomes policy is based on the supposed need to check inflation by means other than deflation but there is little in the record which points to inflation as the factor responsible for strains in the trade balance, let alone other

[1] One estimate for the period 1960–63 shows an increase of 6 per cent in unit costs for the United Kingdom with 12 per cent or more for France, Germany and Italy (NIESR: *Economic Review*, August 1965). For productivity the United Kingdom rate of increase between 1961 and 1964 was rather less than in Germany, almost as much as in France and more than in the United States (*Economist*, 7 August 1965).

items in the current account. On a broad view the case is as unconvincing for the 1960s as for the recovery period or the 1950s.

This conclusion can be supported at several points. If it is assumed that the behaviour of the trade balance depends primarily on the level of costs, the evidence just summarised in the comment on incomes policy (pp. 60–1) corroborates the data presented in the critique of devaluation (pp. 48–9): over the whole period a realistic view does not suggest that inflationary pressures have operated to raise costs above world levels. It could also be maintained that deflationary policy was itself liable to raise costs and had in fact operated in this way (p. 60) while yet another difficulty is the very loose relationship observable between unit costs and export performance (pp. 50–1).

Apart from costs, however, the behaviour of the trade balance may reflect other pressures: demand inflation may be equally potent in restricting the flow of exports or attracting heavy imports. During the earlier post-war years (perhaps for a decade) when the United Kingdom's industrial output was limited by physical capacity, it was not unreasonable to assume that a reduction in domestic demand would help exports (the effect on imports was likely to be small since at the time they were tightly restricted by direct controls). Later the proposition became more doubtful when it was realised that deflation was likely to react unfavourably on productivity and costs but there was still the possibility that 'stop–go' policies might be needed in order to relieve the strain of heavy imports attributable to 'over-heating of the economy'. This implies that an expansionist trend will upset the trade balance.

Such a view hardly accords with the facts. As already seen, it is wholly inapplicable to the earliest post-war crises: in 1947 the operative factor was the deficit of the overseas sterling area superimposed on the impact of convertibility, in 1949 the dollar shortage (again of the overseas sterling area), in 1951 a highly adverse movement in the terms of trade. Nor does it fit the facts very closely in 1955 (when disequilibrium was more marked for the invisibles than for the trade balance) or in 1957 (when there was a near-balance for exports and imports). The hypothesis that expansion in the economy creates an excessive import surplus must therefore rest on the experience of 1961 and 1964. In each of these years import volume rose substantially: in each case, too, heavy imports were associated with a sharp increase in stocks.

The fact of stock-piling is significant although the relationship between imports and stocks is not always clear. For a country like the United Kingdom, dependent on foreign raw materials, rapid growth may quickly attract imports as production rises but initially at least stocks may be run down, to be restored later (perhaps only in part) by heavier imports. Alternatively, the trend for imports and stocks may not register current production needs but the results of changes, or prospective changes, in import controls: at such times over-importing (i.e. imports at a rate well above current usage) is not unlikely.

Although definitive conclusions would be risky, some points are clear. In 1960 much of the increase in stocks was for imports on which controls had just been relaxed and this increase probably accounted for a large part of the adverse balance recorded in that year: it could be said that there was over-importing since the offtake from these stocks obviated any further increase in imports during the next two years. In 1964 conditions were different and even more complex: stocks may have needed replenishment and production was at a record level while there were also exceptional factors such as a steel strike (which necessitated imports of steel), a sharp rise in commodity prices, and the general election (with the prospect that controls would be re-imposed).

Even in the 1960s, therefore, inflationary pressures on the demand side do not fully explain weakness in the trade balance. The import surplus for 1964 suggests the contrary since it demonstrates very forcibly the variety of the factors which may operate. There was first, the expansion factor represented by an exceptionally high growth rate (6 per cent); next, heavy imports of steel because of strikes in the home industry; additionally, stock-piling in anticipation of import controls; and finally, rising import prices.[1] In this one case, therefore, there were factors derived from the domestic economy (expansion *and* contraction), from the world economy and of political rather than economic origins. With such diversity the import surplus cannot be ascribed merely to growth with its attendant pressures.

Criticism of the inflation diagnosis can also be based on quite different grounds. It may not be true that United Kingdom exports are over-priced and there is little reason to think that demand inflation has attracted unduly heavy imports or has erupted in constant crises but it is conceivable that exports have been non-competitive because of defective design or marketing. The evidence for this theory is inconclusive since different methods of statistical analysis appear to yield different results: it would thus require better proof than has so far been adduced to show that exports have been hampered by technical or commercial factors. There is also evidence to the contrary. It would generally be conceded that American technology and salesmanship are second to none yet during the later 1950s the United States share of world exports fell to about the same extent as that of the United Kingdom; again, when discrimination against dollar goods ended, the United States share of the sterling Commonwealth market showed no appreciable increase. Such facts at least demonstrate the need for careful testing of claims which purport to compare competitive status.

No less clear is the need for caution in drawing conclusions from the whole body of data. There are at least two distinct theories (each supported by *some* evidence) which could explain weakness in the trade balance. Without adopting either as correct, the implications for policy should be recognised: if such weakness derives from technical or

[1] Higher import prices accounted for £200 million of the adverse trade balance (£500 million).

commercial factors rather than from prices or demand, a conventional deflationary policy aimed at reducing export prices or the pull of the home market would be irrelevant and an incomes policy equally so.

A full appraisal should allow also for the impact of deflation on the invisibles. Some improvement might be expected in the investment income account since payments would probably be reduced while there would be no direct impact on receipts: the gain would be largely the resultant of a reduction in the profits payable on direct investment and an increase in the interest payable on the sterling balances. The limitations of deflationary policy, however, become further apparent when it is realised that such measures are wholly ineffective in restricting Government expenditure overseas. If this expenditure exceeds the import surplus (as in the 1960s) deflation involves sacrifice (perhaps heavy sacrifice) in an attempt to reduce a relatively small debit without any saving on a much bigger one.

It now begins to look as if the crucial issue of diagnosis cannot easily be resolved. After a review of successive attempts to deal with it, the conclusion may be that none is fully acceptable. The inflation theory (in its variant forms) lacks convincing evidence and may be adjudged not proven; it is also largely irrelevant to the capital account and neglects the overseas sterling area. The approach via war losses is even harder to reconcile with the facts and in any case was of transient rather than permanent validity. Only the dollar shortage (while it lasted) seemed to offer a basis for a comprehensive diagnosis with due allowance for capital movements and the impact of the overseas sterling area on the reserves. But the dollar shortage disappeared at the end of the 1950s while in the early 1960s the problem of sterling seemed to become even more acute.

Perhaps the problem is too complex to admit of a simple diagnosis or a single remedy: this conclusion emerges from a study of the current balance. The new model balance is not homogeneous: its components may move in opposite directions and they respond to different stimuli. There is thus no reason to suppose that policy measures such as devaluation or deflation or an incomes policy (all primarily relevant to visible trade) can operate effectively on the diverse categories which make up the total.

A further complication has also to be examined. Even a policy calculated to keep the current balance in good trim may fail. In the United States the creation of a current surplus has not eliminated external strains, apparent from the loss of reserves. A similar result is much more probable for the United Kingdom since such a surplus is unlikely to replenish the reserves: moreover, reserves and liabilities are governed by other factors. In the next chapter these factors will be identified through study of the capital account.

CHAPTER FOUR

The Capital Account of the Sterling Area

The character of the post-war sterling problem was in part determined by relationships on capital account which in one form or another had long been features of the sterling system. From early in the 19th century the United Kingdom had exported capital to the rest of the world; in the 20th century these exports were largely concentrated on what is now the sterling area. As a result the United Kingdom built up substantial overseas investments while less-developed countries had recourse to the London market for their capital needs.

On the other hand much short-term capital was held in London. Overseas sterling countries, which normally maintained their external reserves as London balances, used them to finance imports from sterling sources or to obtain exchange for imports from other sources: the balances were sustained by capital receipts as well as by export proceeds. Similar procedures applied in the case of other countries which kept balances in London for purposes of trade or finance.

All these balances were liable to fluctuate for various reasons. Sterling countries in deficit on current account often found their reserves heavily depleted, though capital imports sometimes offset this trend. Fluctuations in the balances of non-sterling countries were perhaps rather less dependent on trade and more frequently due to short-term capital movements, occasionally motivated by a failure of confidence.

Since the war the pattern has been modified in several respects. The United Kingdom lost, and later regained, its creditor status; the overseas sterling area attracted heavy imports of capital from the United Kingdom and the United States; much dollar capital was invested in the United Kingdom itself; and at times short-term capital movements (inwards or outwards) assumed massive proportions. Each of these factors had a bearing on the post-war problem.

i. THE UNITED KINGDOM'S CREDITOR STATUS

Any attempt to delineate the United Kingdom's creditor status over a period is hampered by the paucity of published data. Long-term investment overseas just before the war has generally been estimated at £4000–5000 million: it now looks as if the total should be nearer the upper limit.[1] Since wartime disposals of certain holdings amounted to hardly more than £1000 million, it is clear that the great bulk of the investment remained intact after the war. During the early post-war years there was some further liquidation (largely in South America and China but also in certain Commonwealth countries): these post-war disposals perhaps accounted for another £500 million.

There is thus no evidence for the view (current for years after the war) that the United Kingdom had lost all or even the greater part of its overseas investments: at least three-quarters of the total (say, £3500 million) was still available. On this basis the suggestion that the creation of the sterling balances during the war had made the country the world's largest debtor is equally unfounded: net indebtedness appears to have been relatively small, perhaps not much more than £500 million. The widespread acceptance of such notions must have damaged confidence in sterling and a further adverse factor was the failure to realise how soon wartime losses were made good by new investment, on a scale hitherto unknown, after the war.

[1] The 1962 official figure of £8000 million would include some £4000 million for post-war investment. With disposals during and just after the war at about £1500 million, the pre-war total on this basis would have been of the order of £5500 million but a correction should be made to allow for the incidence of devaluation on dollar holdings and for the higher post-war market values of portfolio holdings.

This period is better documented, with official estimates for annual capital exports: the cumulative total for the years 1946–64 was nearly £5000 million.[1] The magnitude of the figure is best appreciated when it realised that within a period of under twenty years investment abroad was (in monetary terms) as much as the pre-war accumulation of over a century.

The results are evident in the survey of external assets and liabilities recently published by the Bank of England: this shows long-term private investment abroad at £8000 million in 1962.[2] The Bank's figures are incomplete in that they exclude (*inter alia*) direct investment by British banks and insurance companies (apart from insurance companies operating in the United States), and the basis of valuation is somewhat unsatisfactory: although portfolio investment is listed at its market value, the bulk of the total represents direct investment at 'book values'. Almost certainly these notional values grossly understate the true or current value: on a more realistic basis the figure might quite possibly be as much as double the book value.[3] If the Bank's estimates for direct investment were raised by no more than 50 per cent, all overseas investments (portfolio and direct) in 1962 could be valued at about £10,000 million.

A later estimate has been published for 1964. The total at the end of that year was put at approximately £10,000 million (excluding Government assets overseas): this figure comprised nearly £4000 million in portfolio investment and £6000 million in direct investment at book values.[4]

[1] Estimates for the years 1952–61 were published in *Economic Trends*, June 1962; thereafter the figures have been published in the annual balance of payments statements. For the period 1946–51 there is an estimate in the Radcliffe Committee's *Report* (para 736). The figure quoted is for private investment only.

[2] Bank of England, *Quarterly Bulletin*, March 1964.

[3] See A. R. Conan: *A Note on the New Estimates of Direct Investment* (Bulletin of Oxford University Institute of Economics and Statistics, May 1964).

[4] Statements by Chancellor of Exchequer in Budget Speech (7 April 1965) and by Chief Secretary to the Treasury (reported in *Financial Times*, 26 April 1965).

An estimate in the £8000–10,000 million range would afford ample cover for the major items on the debit side which arose as a result of the war: these include sterling balances of approximately £3000 million and Government external debt of some £1300 million (net). But in addition there is now a debit of £4000 million for long-term investment in the United Kingdom: this debit is for capital (mainly from the United States) invested in business undertakings, which for the most part has been received since the war. Thus, of the three debit items, the largest is of post-war, rather than wartime, origin.

Even with overseas assets under-valued in the official estimates, there is a net surplus for these categories (without adding in the gold reserves). The position is set out in the statement below.

CREDITOR STATUS OF THE UNITED KINGDOM
£ million

	1962	1964
Overseas Investments:		
Portfolio	3,000	4,000
Direct	5,000	6,000
Total (private)	8,000	10,000
Investment in UK	3,000	4,000
UK Government Debt	1,500	1,300
Sterling Balances	2,900	3,100

The net balance for all items, long-term and short-term, enumerated by the Bank of England for 1962 was £1600 million (including the gold reserves) but the Bank expressed the view that this must be regarded as an under-estimate: there can thus be no risk in putting the total for that year at some £2000 million in round figures. An alternative estimate based on the evidence that direct investment is grossly understated by the Bank, would suggest a net credit of about £3000 million.

It seems probable that in the early 1950s the United Kingdom regained its status as a creditor country and it is clear that during the next ten years or so creditor status was strongly reinforced. The record thus negatives the suggestion that since the war capital exports have been relatively small. This suggestion, based on the belief that post-war capital exports represented merely a transfer from the United Kingdom to other countries of capital which it had itself imported, is inconsistent with the data published by the Bank of England. If (as is generally accepted) the United Kingdom was a debtor country after the war and if (as appears from the Bank's estimates) there is now a substantial net surplus of assets, the transition from debtor to creditor status was effected by exports of capital which were not re-exports. There is thus adequate evidence to show that the United Kingdom has in recent years been able to invest abroad from its own resources.

The exact amount of the present surplus is not perhaps material but the transition from debit to credit can reasonably be taken as evidence of post-war recovery on capital account. Since it was held at the end of the war (and much later) that the loss of overseas investments and the accumulation of large external liabilities denoted weakness, the elimination of such weakness by heavy capital exports should have strengthened sterling.

This view has sometimes been controverted. It has been maintained that status as an international creditor or debtor is not of great significance and that instead of rebuilding overseas investments a larger part of the current surplus should have been utilised in adding to the reserves. The proposition was rejected by the Radcliffe Committee in the following terms.

First, it is one of the objectives of the United Kingdom Government's policy to contribute to the more rapid development of Commonwealth countries. This being so, it cannot discourage the investment which has contributed so notably to past development.

Secondly, even from the standpoint of self-interest investment in overseas countries is urgent and valuable. Much of it is in countries that are at once important suppliers of the United Kingdom and large purchasers of United Kingdom goods. Investment in these countries contributes to an expansion or cheapening in the supplies of goods which the United Kingdom imports and generates additional export opportunities. . . .

Finally, the fact that it might be preferable to have less investment in long-term assets and a faster build-up of the reserves does not mean that the Government need only tighten its control over capital exports to make the reserves increase. The variables that go to make up the balance of payments react on one another in so many different ways that it is very hard to predict how a change in the total balance would be divided between the constituent elements. . . .[1]

The Committee's conclusion on this topic is of contemporary interest since in 1965 steps were taken to restrict overseas investment. It should, however, be amplified on one point. Treasury witnesses had testified that a major policy objective was to improve the ratio between reserves and liabilities ('they appeared to be comparatively indifferent which form the improvement took'): the Committee itself seemed doubtful whether intensified restrictions on capital exports would benefit the reserves as the main reaction might be on the sterling balances. The issue can be clarified by reference to the distribution of investment between sterling and non-sterling countries: the former accounted for more than half of the total and, non-sterling investment being already restricted, the effect of further restrictions would probably be slight. There is here a parallel with the sector distribution of the surplus on current account: just as this surplus (derived from sterling countries) does not replenish the reserves, so capital exports being predominantly to such countries, have likewise a limited effect in the reverse direction.

The Committee made no attempt to evaluate the impact of capital imports into the United Kingdom although in view of their magnitude (as noted earlier) an appraisal would have been relevant to the issue. In the first instance these capital imports replenish the reserves (since they are

[1] *Report*, paras 741–43.

virtually all from non-sterling countries) but that is only the initial impact: the record shows that the amount now payable as investment income puts a severe strain on current invisibles while quite possibly there may also be an adverse effect on visible trade. Thus the total impact on the reserves is the resultant of a once-for-all credit on capital account and a continuing debit on current account. Under such conditions (and mindful of the qualifications in the preceding paragraph) it is arguable whether the reserves might not benefit more from restrictions on imports than on exports of capital.

So far this proposition has not found acceptance and in view of the decision to restrict capital exports it may be useful to summarise here the main results of the post-war outflow. Estimates of magnitude have been given above: the results should also be stated in concrete terms.

As already indicated, heavy capital exports have enabled the United Kingdom to regain its creditor status. This must be accounted significant if only because opinion abroad rated sterling largely on the assumption that the United Kingdom as a debtor country was insolvent, and the pound therefore vulnerable. The recovery of creditor status in fact removes one of the main supports of the war losses theory.

Next, there is the safeguard of ample second-line reserves which can be utilised in an emergency. Although overseas investments are not always immediately realisable, it has been found in two world wars that they can be mobilised to supplement other sources of foreign exchange. Nor are such operations necessarily confined to wartime emergencies. In 1956, for example, dollar securities were pledged against a loan in the United States while in the same year the sale of a single concern (the Trinidad Oil Company) replenished the reserves to the extent of nearly 200 million dollars.

Finally, since the reserve position registers current as well as capital transactions, their interrelationships should not be overlooked. The impact on visible trade is indeterminate but possibly substantial: exports were (probably) sustained directly by overseas investment and indirectly because this investment buttressed the reserves of recipient countries (especially in the sterling area). Nor is there any substance in the claim that post-war capital exports have yielded scanty returns: gross investment income at perhaps four times the pre-war figure reinforces the current balance. If, without large capital exports, investment income after the war had risen to only £400 million per annum (as against the actual figure of £900 million) there would now be a gap of £500 million each year (much more than any attributable to the trade deficit).

A policy aimed at the restriction of long-term capital exports (either to increase the reserves or for other reasons) is therefore questionable: the net gain from such a policy must be dubious since overseas investment fortifies the capital account as well as the current balance and puts little pressure on the reserves.

The impact is very different in the case of short-term capital movements. These (whether inwards or outwards) are usually confined to foreign-owned funds: exports of capital in this category must therefore be distinguished from overseas investment by United Kingdom citizens. Furthermore, short-term capital is essentially volatile as it moves not in a steady flow but intermittently and its movements are often quickly reversed.

Such characteristics can produce harmful repercussions. An inward movement of funds is usually from non-sterling sources[1] and in the first instance adds to the reserves but the accrual may be only temporary as the funds may soon be withdrawn: since any withdrawal is likely to be directed to non-sterling countries, it involves a reduction in the reserves. Thus, although a short-term capital inflow seems to be a cheap way of replenishing the pool (as the interest payable is likely to be low) the benefit will be illusory if the loss of the funds proves embarrassing.

The post-war record includes several notable instances of large-scale losses: these (rather than the current balance)

[1] Additions to London balances by overseas sterling countries are not here included as short-term inflows.

were decisive in the crises of 1947 and 1949 while the experience was repeated in 1957 and again (twice) in the early 1960s. On at least one occasion (1960) a massive inflow proved useful because it offset weakness in the current account. Short-term capital movements must therefore be included with the United Kingdom's exports and imports of long-term capital as determinants of the reserves (additional to the current balance). The list is not exhaustive: other determinants will be investigated in later sections.

ii. DATA FOR THE OVERSEAS SECTOR

Heavy imports of capital into overseas sterling countries have been a prominent feature of the post-war scene. To a large extent these imports were the counterpart of capital exports from the United Kingdom but there was also a substantial inflow from other sources.[1]

In the past close banking and trading connections facilitated the flow of capital from the United Kingdom to what is now the overseas sterling area. After the war certain new measures reinforced these connections: the export of capital through market issues or by direct investment was in the main limited to sterling countries as investment elsewhere was restricted.

The results can be stated more precisely. Official estimates for the years 1946–64 allocate £2900 million to the overseas sterling area and £1900 million to the rest of the world: thus almost two-thirds of the total was channelled into the former sector. This represented an increase as compared with pre-war since in 1938 the sterling area accounted for less than half the recorded holdings of overseas investments.

Within the sterling area virtually all the United Kingdom's capital exports went to the Commonwealth or the Middle East oil producers. The latter group, a comparatively new field for investment, has probably absorbed over £500

[1] A detailed statement will be found in A. R. Conan: *Capital Imports into Sterling Countries* (Macmillan, 1960).

million since the war. Countries in the sterling Commonwealth, where before the war the United Kingdom had invested about £2000 million, have in post-war years received at least as much again from this source.

The United Kingdom, however, is no longer the only source of capital supply for the overseas sterling area. Although member countries still draw on it for their capital needs, they now look elsewhere as well, and particularly to the dollar area. The International Bank has financed many development projects in under-developed countries and they have also had the benefit of Aid from the United States: in addition to free grants, loans were arranged under Aid Programmes. Business capital also was imported from the United States: for this category the main recipients were Australia, South Africa and certain colonial territories while there was substantial American investment in the Middle East oil group. Other sources of capital supply have been of much less importance but funds have been received from various countries, mainly in Europe.

All these items amounted in the aggregate to a very large sum. Apart from grants under Aid Programmes, the overseas sterling area has since the war imported as long-term capital some £3000 million from the United Kingdom and even more from non-sterling countries. The post-war inflow from all sources was probably in monetary terms about three times as great as the pre-war total received over a period of perhaps a hundred years.

A capital flow on such a scale must have wide repercussions. No attempt can be made here to state these repercussions in detail but the impact on London as the centre of the sterling system will be investigated in due course. The impact can be traced via the overseas sector to the sterling balances and the central reserves: these in turn registered changes in the balance of payments for this sector.

The initial impulse came from the mounting indebtedness of overseas sterling countries. A contrast with the United Kingdom at once becomes evident: the latter incurred debt during the war and as a result of the war, the former during the process of economic development after the war. The contrast suggests that even heavy indebtedness should not by itself damage a country's economic potential or impair its balance of payments.

This conclusion should be checked against the record. An increase in external debt necessarily brings a corresponding increase on the debit side of the investment account. The extent to which the debit can be regarded as onerous depends largely on the trend for the trade balance: no strain need arise if the balance is improved by the investment which has to be serviced. On such a test the record for the overseas sterling area as a whole shows little sign of an appropriate response. Data for the visible balance are summarised in the table below:

VISIBLE BALANCE OF OVERSEAS STERLING AREA

£ million

	Balance* with United Kingdom	Balance* with Non-sterling Area	Gold Output
1950–54 (average)	−5	164	186
1955–59 (average)	−71	−139	248
1960	−49	−454	298
1961	−28	−236	320
1962	50	−255	349
1963	32	−161	376
1964	79	−419	398

* Merchandise trade only.

Source: United Kingdom balance of payments statistics.

One feature of the table is the marked deterioration for the trade account. Starting from overall surplus in the early 1950s, this deterioration culminated ten years later, with some improvement subsequently. The balance with the United Kingdom has shown relatively little change: the margin between exports and imports is small. The adverse trend has been in trade with the non-sterling world: here the 1950s saw the emergence of a heavy deficit and in the early 1960s this averaged as much as £300 million per annum.

The adverse trade balance was in the main offset by higher gold production in sterling countries: although the increase in output was chiefly due to technical factors, it was partly dependent on external capital since the development of new mines in South Africa (the main producer) required more finance than was available from domestic sources. Even with gold included as a credit, however, the visible balance has failed to produce the surplus needed for equilibrium in the current account as a whole: the deficit for invisibles (nearly all due to the return on investment) now amounts to about £800 million per annum. Thus, with a highly adverse trend for trade and with invisibles only to a small extent covered by receipts from gold, the current account of the overseas sterling area has for years been heavily adverse. For the period 1960–64 the cumulative deficit was no less than £3000 million, about one-half being with non-sterling countries.

It seems probable that the deficit was largely occasioned by the capital inflow: under such conditions imports would be maintained at a high level with a corresponding bill for shipping costs as well as heavier payments on investment account. But the reactions extended even farther. In addition to its impact on the current account, the flow of capital sustained the sterling balances of each recipient country (although they were depleted by the current deficit). Moreover, while the deficit with non-sterling countries constituted a drain on the central reserves, the pool was simultaneously replenished by capital receipts from such countries. These reactions will be treated in the two following sections.

iii. THE STERLING BALANCES

The existence of large sterling balances originally created during the war was long considered to be one of the post-war problems which the United Kingdom had to solve if sterling was to be re-established as a key-currency. Two related issues can be distinguished. In the first place this indebtedness was mainly responsible for the loss of the United Kingdom's creditor status after the war. Secondly, since the sterling balances were regarded as short-term debt, they seemed to involve an undue disparity between quick reserves and sight liabilities.

Data bearing on the first point have been presented in section i of this chapter; the second point can be illustrated by figures for the reserves and liabilities. In 1939 the sterling balances totalled only £500 million; in that year, too, these liabilities were covered by gold reserves of approximately the same amount. By 1945 the gold reserves were hardly greater than before the war while the liabilities had risen seven-fold.

Earlier discussion of the problem was directed towards possible methods of liquidating the debt. Where the balances were far greater than would be needed for use as external reserves, the United Kingdom Government recorded in the Washington Loan Agreement its intention of negotiating a settlement: so far as sterling countries were concerned, this was to provide for 'adjustment' of the balances as a contribution to the liquidation of war and post-war indebtedness. In the event no such agreements were concluded although in the case of India and Pakistan part of the debt was extinguished by offsetting it against certain items due to the United Kingdom.

The figure of some £3500 million (old series) outstanding at the end of the war was thus accepted as a debt for repayment in due course. The published series plainly suggests that it has not been possible to make any progress towards the objective: in the early 1960s the amount outstanding was still the same as in 1945.

On further analysis this conclusion must be modified. Although the balances appear impervious to change, there have been fundamental changes which are not evident in the totals. Several points call for mention.

First, the burden of the debt in real terms has been reduced as a result of inflation. As world price levels have risen by about 75 per cent since the end of the war, the price factor has operated to an extent which must be regarded as significant. On the other hand, with higher interest rates, the cost of servicing the balances has increased: between 1950 and 1956, without any appreciable change in the amount outstanding, service payments rose from £33 million to £114 million, although by the end of the 1950s the figure was once again under £100 million.

Next, there have been large changes from time to time in the composition of the total. Primarily, these involved the balances held by non-sterling countries: during the first post-war decade the sub-total for this category had fallen by one-half and they were considered to be no greater than normal working balances (in real terms they were appreciably less than before the war). There had not been any comparable reduction in the total held by sterling countries: although the balances of independent Commonwealth countries fell heavily, a large increase was recorded for the Colonies and the Middle East oil countries.

The extent to which these groups displayed opposite trends which combined to give a total substantially unchanged is shown by the figures for the six years 1951–56:[1]

	£ million
Non-sterling countries	−400
Independent Commonwealth	−500
Colonial Territories	+650
Middle East countries	+250

Although by the mid-1950s the balances of non-sterling countries had been reduced to manageable proportions, they did not remain at that level. A massive influx of short-term capital (largely due to the weakness of the United States dollar) raised them from under £700 million at the end of 1956 to twice that figure at the end of 1960. Subsequently the efflux of these funds reduced the total to approximately £800 million in 1962.

Over the post-war period as a whole the fluctuations in non-sterling balances were in marked contrast with the stability of the balances held by sterling countries: the latter,

[1] Figures from memorandum submitted by the Bank of England to the Radcliffe Committee reprinted in *The Rationale of the Sterling Area* by A. R. Conan (Macmillan, 1961).

nearly £2500 million at the end of the war, have not since varied by more than £400 million on either side of that figure. This stability was partly attributable to the absence of large short-term capital movements; in part, too, it was the resultant of opposite trends on current and capital account.

Detailed analysis of these trends must start from the United Kingdom's current surplus with other sterling countries: this by itself absorbs an equivalent amount of sterling held by these countries. The cumulative surplus from 1946 to 1964 was just under £5000 million: it is thus clear that the surplus operating alone would have liquidated the total outstanding in 1945.

Another factor which drew down the balances was the current deficit of the overseas sterling area with the non-sterling world: for the period 1950–64 the cumulative deficit amounted to £4750 million and this figure should possibly be increased to take account of the years 1946–49.

On the other hand purchases of gold by the United Kingdom from other sterling countries have been substantial over the years: as such purchases are paid for in sterling, these transactions create *new* balances. Gold purchases have probably exceeded £3000 million and sterling to an equivalent extent has been credited to the accounts of the gold-producing countries.

An even more potent factor which operated to sustain the balances was the flow of long-term capital. Here (as detailed in the preceding section) the outflow from the United Kingdom to overseas sterling countries as well as their imports from non-sterling sources must be brought into the reckoning: the total amounted to at least £6000 million.

In the aggregate, therefore, the balances of the overseas sterling area have been depleted by the debit on current account (net of gold sales) and replenished by capital receipts. The capital inflow not only neutralised the current deficit but also transformed the character of the balances. At the end of the war they represented (for the United Kingdom) debts incurred mainly for war needs; these were subsequently repaid. They were replaced by new liabilities fully covered by assets such as gold and overseas investments.

Once the true character of the existing sterling balances has been established, they cannot be treated as comparable to war debts and the burden involved cannot be assessed without taking into account the assets held against them: in other words, a distinction must be made between liabilities which are fully covered by assets and those which are not. For the United Kingdom the balances of sterling countries are liabilities in the sense that a bank's deposits are liabilities (and were created in much the same way). A statement of international credits and debits (analogous to a bank's balance sheet) showing a surplus of credits (as in the Bank of England's estimates summarised on p. 70) gives the true perspective.

Viewed in this way the sterling balances no longer, as at the end of the war, advertise the United Kingdom's debtor status; on the contrary, the figures when analysed demonstrate how creditor status was regained. The analysis also suggests that the process involved *pari passu* a deterioration in the creditor status of other countries and a breakdown of the total for the overseas sterling area shows where it occurred. The summary table below gives details for certain groups of countries in selected years:

LONDON BALANCES OF STERLING COUNTRIES

£ million

	India, Pakistan and Ceylon	Australia, New Zealand and S. Africa	Middle Eastern Countries	The Colonial Territories	Total*
1945	1352	294	—	411	2327
1950	787	640	19	719	2497
1955	704	313	169	1280	2764
1960	198	285	368	1269†	2478

* Including other countries. † 1957.

Source: Bank of England: *Quarterly Bulletin*, December 1963, and (for the Colonial Territories) *New Contributions to Economic Statistics* (HMSO, 1959).

The main feature of the table is the elimination of the enormous wartime accumulation of sterling formerly held by India, Pakistan and Ceylon, which accounted for over half of the total for sterling countries at the end of the war: within fifteen years more than £1000 million has been repaid. It is hardly too much to say that this repayment, in conjunction with the repayment of £700 million to non-sterling countries between 1946 and 1956 (a total reduction of nearly £2000 million), virtually disposed of the wartime sterling balances.

Among the other groups the trend has generally been in the opposite direction. Except for Australia, New Zealand and South Africa taken together, where there was little change, the 1960 figures were far above the end-war level. (The same is true in the aggregate for other sterling countries not shown in the table.) Thus in so far as the balances of sterling countries now constitute a problem for the United Kingdom, it has since the war been accentuated, not eased, apart from the Indian group.

For one group in particular, the Middle East countries, the figures clearly testify to the emergence of the problem as a post-war phenomenon. At the end of the war these countries (all of minor importance) had no sterling funds: by 1960 their London balances were well above the total for Australia, New Zealand and South Africa taken together. The increase here reflects primarily the investment directed towards the development of the oil resources in the countries concerned.

There is a marked contrast with the group comprising Australia, New Zealand and South Africa. The fact that London balances for this group taken as a whole showed virtually no change over the period 1945–60 must be related to the fact that during the period these three countries together imported about £2000 million of capital from abroad. The import of capital therefore merely sufficed to cover the cumulative deficit on current account.

The Colonial Territories conform to the pattern displayed by the Middle East oil countries. At the end of the war the colonial balances were not exceptionally large (only £400 million) but by 1957 they had risen to nearly £1300 million. It was often assumed that the increase represented investment by the Colonies in the United Kingdom but in fact the reverse was true. Post-war additions to these balances were in no sense earned since the cumulative total for the current account of the Colonial Territories showed a deficit: to set against the deficit, however, there were capital receipts (Government loans, grants and business capital) which exceeded £1000 million. Although the balances were invested in London, there was no *net* investment since for the most part they represented funds transferred to the Colonies by the United Kingdom.

Overall, the breakdown reveals that with a total substantially unchanged since the war there have been diverse trends as between different groups in the overseas sterling area: for one group a large reduction, for two others a large increase and for a fourth group little change. Given these trends it may be asked whether now, as at the end of the war, the balances constitute a problem on which action is needed.

Expressed in this way the query is ambiguous. The main issue concerns the magnitude of the total. For the United Kingdom such a large mass of indebtedness may well be onerous not merely because it suggests an unfavourable reserve ratio but also because the service of the debt involves payment abroad of about £100 million per annum: in that sense the balances may be inconveniently large. Alternatively, the point can be taken in relation to the other countries concerned: for them the balances would be excessive if much above what is needed as a reserve or otherwise.

The proposition that the balances are surplus to requirements, even if true at the end of the war, now seems untenable. The Bank of England, in a paper submitted to the Radcliffe Committee, assessed the figures in 1956. It was then judged that the holdings of non-sterling countries had been reduced to 'a natural (perhaps low) working level': at the end of 1964 they were not significantly greater. As regards the independent Commonwealth countries, the Bank considered that none except India held sterling much above a reasonable minimum; since then India's balances have fallen heavily while there have been large fluctuations but no sustained increase in the holdings of Australia, New Zealand and South Africa. This leaves only two groups with holdings which may be excessive: the Middle East oil countries and those which until recently were designated the Colonial Territories.

The figures for the oil countries are not perhaps of overwhelming magnitude, accounting for about one-tenth of the total: they could fall as development proceeds but up to the end of 1962 there was no sign that they had reached their peak. On the other hand the balances of the Colonial or ex-Colonial Territories, which in the later 1950s accounted for over one-third of the total, have been under some strain although a heavy reduction in Africa has been neutralised by an increase in the Far East. For both groups it should be noted that a large accumulation of sterling does not necessarily imply the existence of surplus balances but rather denotes an under-developed financial system: these funds (used for operations connected with currency, banking and public finance) are held in London because of limited investment facilities in the territories concerned.

On a broad view there appears to be little scope for any general repayment as had earlier been proposed. The independent Commonwealth countries have rarely been able to maintain an adequate margin over minimum needs: at one time or another Australia, New Zealand, South Africa and India (to name only the most notable cases) have drawn down their holdings to a point where emergency measures were required to prevent further depletion: much the same is true for other countries in the group. Such emergencies reflect the instability which characterises the balance of payments in a primary producing country: experience shows that in order to overcome them, it is necessary to hold relatively large external assets.

If the scaling-down of 'excess balances' as contemplated at the end of the war is impracticable and the colonial balances must be maintained unless there are radical changes in the financial institutions of the territories concerned, the conclusion appears to be that the existing balances are not, for the most part, surplus to requirements. The Radcliffe Committee adopted this view, expressing the opinion that any attempt to effect a rapid reduction in the total would be inadvisable: 'Repayment of sterling balances in so far as they constitute the central reserves of other countries or the working balances of overseas central banks, would tend to reduce the liquidity of overseas monetary systems. . . . We should therefore refrain from seizing too eagerly on the opportunity of extinguishing short-term debts as a means of strengthening the pound sterling.'[1]

From the United Kingdom standpoint post-war history suggests that the mere size of the balances is of minor significance: the impact derives from their character. The balances of sterling countries have been on the whole relatively stable; those of non-sterling countries highly unstable. This contrast, given the mechanism of the sterling system, is the key to the problem.

The volatile character of the non-sterling group is no doubt partly due to the fact that for the most part (two-thirds at end-1963) these balances are privately held and may largely comprise short-term capital; sterling area balances are mostly held by central banks and other official bodies, only one-fifth being in private hands. These official balances are less likely to be affected by speculative movements or a failure of confidence: they are not in fact balances as ordinarily understood, more than half of the total being invested in British Government stocks and most of the remainder in Treasury bills. The distinction is of practical importance because a reduction in the balances of non-sterling countries due to an outflow of short-term capital will probably involve a reduction in the reserves: the crises of 1957, 1961 and 1964 originated in this way. Such trans-

[1] *Report*, para 662.

actions are unusual in the case of the overseas sterling area and would be innocuous if they involved only repatriation of capital from the United Kingdom.

It can also be accounted a stabilising factor that the balances of sterling countries now constitute a larger proportion of the total (four-fifths) than at the end of the war (two-thirds) while in absolute terms the non-sterling balances have been heavily reduced: on the other hand this factor may have been offset by the relaxation of exchange controls and the introduction of convertibility at the end of the 1950s. But in any case it would be incorrect to treat the total as a mass of short-term indebtedness which makes the pound sensitive to external pressures: the liabilities are nearly all inert with perhaps not much more than £500 million which can be regarded as volatile.

The conclusion must modify the accepted view as to the cover required for this indebtedness. As already noted, the United Kingdom now has a large net surplus of assets over liabilities (all classes): in the following section reference will be made to the reserve ratio in the narrower sense of the quick assets held against short-term liabilities.

iv. THE RESERVES

The maintenance of balances in London has a parallel with another function of the United Kingdom as banker for the overseas sterling area: although these balances are the external reserves of member countries, the centralised reserves held by the United Kingdom in London supply the international currency used by the whole system. On the banking analogy the sterling balances may be designated liabilities of the United Kingdom while the reserves are regarded as assets: banking practice would accordingly require a proper ratio between the latter and the former. The post-war history of sterling is largely concerned with the attempt to maintain this ratio and some points in the record must now be examined in detail.

Like other features of the sterling system, the pooling of

international currency reserves was formalised during the war when wartime conditions made it necessary to conserve gold and dollars by ensuring that they were used only for essential needs. A contemporary statement described the dollar pool as follows:

The United Kingdom undertakes to make available to other sterling area countries the dollar exchange which they may currently require to settle unfavourable balances in their dollar transactions. On the other hand, any surplus gold or dollar exchange which such countries may currently acquire from international transactions — or, as in the case of gold, from domestic production or dishoarding — is customarily made available to the United Kingdom.[1]

It has already been seen that soon after the war the dollar deficit imposed a severe strain on the mechanism: as the dollar-earning capacity of the overseas sterling area had been greatly impaired (not least through the reduction in the purchasing power of gold) this sector was no longer in surplus on dollar account and drew heavily on the pool until 1950. Such conditions naturally depressed the level of the reserves in the earlier post-war years.

Although the impact of the dollar problem is now only of historic interest, reference to it may serve to illustrate the practical working of the central reserve system: in particular, it demonstrates the inadequacy of data for the United Kingdom balance of payments as evidence for the strength of the pound. Moreover, the problem is of permanent interest in that it exemplifies the role of the overseas sterling area in relation to the reserves.

This role must be studied in a wider context. The dollar shortage has ended and a large measure of convertibility has been introduced: the dollar problem should accordingly be merged in the broader problem of relationships between the sterling area and non-sterling countries. On the new basis the strength of the pound is governed by the balance of payments between the system and the rest of the world: this balance determines the level of the reserves.

[1] *Federal Reserve Bulletin*, February 1941.

A summary of the statistical data for the current account discloses a highly adverse trend during the 1950s. In the first half of the decade there were large fluctuations between surplus and deficit, with a cumulative surplus of approximately £100 million: since 1955 the current account has been continuously in deficit.

CURRENT TRANSACTIONS WITH NON-STERLING COUNTRIES

£ million

	United Kingdom	Overseas Sterling Area	Total
1950–54 (average)	−175	194	19
1955–59 (average)	−147	−61	−208
1960	−626	−395	−1021
1961	−307	−190	−497
1962	−105	−176	−281
1963	−132	−215	−347
1964	−513	−530	−1043

Source: United Kingdom balance of payments statements (figures for the overseas sterling area include gold as a credit).

The components of the total are significant. The normal United Kingdom deficit with the external world has not on the whole altered much: although with large year-to-year fluctuations, the annual average during the 1950s was approximately £150 million and only in the early 1960s was the shortfall (on occasion) much heavier. The trend for the overseas sterling area was more serious: in the 1950s it had lapsed from surplus to deficit while in the first quinquennium of the 1960s its cumulative deficit almost equalled that of the United Kingdom.

This denotes a major structural change for the sterling system. Formerly the working of the system in relation to the non-sterling world depended on reciprocal links between the United Kingdom and the overseas sterling area: more specifically, the deficit of the former was set against the surplus of the latter. Now (if recent trends persist) the system can no longer function on that basis: the United Kingdom still runs the usual deficit but the overseas sterling area no longer earns a surplus to cover it.

Any failure of the sterling area as a whole to balance its accounts must have a depressive effect on the reserves. The effect was hardly felt during the first half of the 1950s but thereafter became dominant. Data for a recent period will show the results in quantitative terms. During the five years 1958–62[1] the cumulative deficit of the United Kingdom with the non-sterling world amounted to about £1300 million: the corresponding figure for the overseas sterling area exceeded £1000 million. Current transactions thus involved a drain of approximately £2400 million.

Such a trend would in itself have exhausted the reserves but superimposed on it was a wholly new factor: the inflow of long-term capital from non-sterling sources. As the reserves rose during the period stated, the capital inflow effectively neutralised the current deficit. In other words, capital imports are now a main determinant of the reserves.

This again represents a basic structural change. Historically, the status of the pound has often been affected by capital flows. In the long-term category these were mostly *exports* from the United Kingdom and so far as they were destined for the overseas sterling area the impact was slight; there were also short-term capital flows which comprised both inward and outward movements, usually with corresponding changes in the reserves. The post-war novelty has been the *import* of non-sterling capital into both the United Kingdom and other sterling countries: given the scale of these movements and the existence of the pooling system, the impact on the reserves must now be rated as even greater than the impact of short-term capital.

The results for recent years are satisfactory only in the sense that the current deficit did not deplete the reserves. The balance is precarious because a contribution to the pool derived from a capital inflow is not the same as a contribution earned by trade. In the first place capital flows are characteristically unstable and liable to interruption: a

[1] This period has been selected because during it short-term capital movements (including transactions with the IMF) were in the aggregate relatively small.

classic instance is the case of Australia at the end of the 1920s when the cessation of overseas borrowing coincident with a fall in export prices occasioned the devaluation of the Australian pound. Secondly, the process creates at least a contingent liability because the capital may be repatriated: where (as for the sterling area in post-war years) the inflow has comprised mainly business capital for direct investment, repatriation may be embarrassing since the original sum received will grow through reinvestment of profits. Thirdly, there is not merely a contingent but an actual liability for the service of the investment: with business capital this is likely to increase very rapidly through reinvestment. Finally, policy may have to be recast to meet a situation where the reserves are governed by long-term as well as short-term capital flows. The former are probably less volatile than the latter (perhaps because there is not so much scope for the confidence factor) but may be harder to control since long-term capital is not very amenable to changes in Bank rate.

The extent of the potential readjustment cannot be assessed but the prospect further illustrates the problem of policy controls for the new model balance of payments. Moreover, the dominant role of capital movements in sustaining the reserves implies as corollary a relatively minor role for the United Kingdom's current account in this context.

Again data for a specific period will serve to illustrate the point. During the years 1958–63 the current account showed a surplus of nearly £2000 million with the overseas sterling area and a deficit of nearly £1500 million with the non-sterling world. The surplus contributed nothing to the reserves; the deficit involved an equivalent drain. On capital account the United Kingdom exported £1000 million of long-term capital to non-sterling countries and imported long-term capital therefrom to the extent of £1400 million; these transactions thus yielded a balance of £400 million. (For the period as a whole, there was no significant balance of short-term capital movements, heavy imports in 1960 being withdrawn the following year.) In this case, therefore, the deficit on capital account, not the surplus on current account, was the effective agent in replenishing the reserves.

The analysis can be pursued even further. Although the United Kingdom could contribute to the reserves from capital imports, a broader view would show a different picture. During the period stated the overseas sterling area imported no less than £2500 million of long-term capital from non-sterling sources; after deducting the current deficit, there was a balance of £1200 million available for the reserves. For this period at least, therefore, the main increment on capital account (three-quarters of the whole) came from the overseas sector. Moreover, the outturn for the United Kingdom (current and long-term capital transactions) was negative: despite the overall surplus in the current balance and the contribution from capital receipts, the United Kingdom drew heavily on the reserves.

The new balance of payments structure taken with other post-war changes in the capital account calls for some revision of accepted views on the optimum size of the reserves. The issues may be restated here. Three possible cases can be distinguished.

It is sometimes said that reserves must be maintained as an offset against the sterling balances. This view is questionable. Full repayment of the balances is unlikely since they are mostly held as external assets needed for trade or finance. Even if the total (£3000 million in 1964) is much above the corresponding pre-war figure, allowance should be made for higher world price levels: adjusted for current prices, the equivalent of the pre-war total would be nearly £2000 million.

The point should also be considered in relation to the complete balance-sheet of assets and liabilities. The picture is very different from what it was when the balances first came under discussion at the end of the war: the liabilities are now, as they were not then, backed by a substantial net surplus in the form of overseas investments. If it is unrealistic to regard the whole of the balances as fully expendable, these investments (and in particular the portfolio holdings now totalling £4000 million) may properly be included as backing, especially as they have sometimes been mobilised to augment the reserves.

More often it is maintained that a reserve is needed to provide against fluctuations in the current account. This view does not accord with experience: over an extended period, 1948–63, a current deficit coincided with a reduction in the reserves on only two occasions (1951 and 1955). Even in 1964, when the deficit was as much as £400 million, the impact was relatively slight: for the greater part of the year there was no perceptible effect while less than one-quarter of the heavy fall in the reserves during October and November was due to current transactions.

An up-to-date appraisal would be different. With the balance of payments as now constituted, the whole sterling area is constantly in deficit on current account while simultaneously importing large amounts of capital. Under such conditions the role of the reserves is neutral, the deficit being met from capital receipts. A more accurate statement would be based on the need for reserves as a safeguard against the possible interruption of the capital inflow. Recent events have emphasised the risks: United States measures aimed at limiting capital exports must (if effective) impose an equivalent readjustment on the sterling area.

Finally, there is the view which relates the reserves to the sterling balances, stating the relationship in terms of the ratio between short-term liabilities and the quick assets available to cover them. Since the war this ratio has been regarded as crucial: in evidence before the Radcliffe Committee the Treasury went so far as to say that the main policy objective was to improve it.

Until recently attempts to present the ratio in concrete detail have been hampered by inadequate data for its components. On the debit side the figures for the sterling balances were defective. The Radcliffe Committee revealed [1] that the series as then computed (and used as the basis for discussion) did not exhibit a net liability since the totals

[1] *Report*, para 628.

included items for which there were counterparts in the form of liabilities due to the United Kingdom. The defect remained until a new series was introduced in 1963: the total as shown in the revised series was some £500 million less than that previously used. This by itself represented a marked improvement in the reserve ratio as hitherto accepted.

The Radcliffe Committee also pointed out[1] that on the assets side the official figures for the reserves understated the true total: in the main the understatement was due to the exclusion of the balances held by United Kingdom banks overseas for day-to-day working requirements. It has now been disclosed by the Bank of England[2] that in 1962 the claims of the banking system in non-sterling currencies amounted to no less than £1000 million.

The new data transform the reserve situation. A revision of the figure formerly accepted is necessitated not merely by the magnitude of the assets held in the commercial banking system but also because, as the first-line reserves of the system in its international operations, they are freely utilised: they therefore take the strain of any adverse trend in the balance of payments and cannot be omitted in assessing the total reserves available for use.

On the revised basis the ratio of quick reserves to short-term liabilities looks very different. For the post-war period as a whole reserves have generally been shown at approximately £1000 million and the sterling balances at £3500 million: the ratio was thus under 30 per cent. Now, reserves of £2000 million have to be set against net liabilities of £4100 million: on that basis the ratio is almost 50 per cent.

Even this is an understatement. Since the Bank includes as short-term liabilities large holdings (£1000 million) of United Kingdom Government securities (on the ground that they *may* be liquidated at any time) a consistent classification should include among quick assets the official holdings of dollar securities (which *can* be liquidated at any time); such securities were valued in 1964 at nearly £500

[1] *Report*, para 614. [2] *Quarterly Bulletin*, March 1964.

million.[1] With these added, the quick reserves would total £2500 million as against liabilities of £4000 million. A realistic liquidity ratio, therefore, can reasonably be taken as 60 per cent, twice the figure formerly used.

By ordinary banking standards a ratio of that order would be fully adequate, especially as the liabilities are not for the most part exceptionally volatile. Liabilities of this kind do not need to be backed pound for pound by *liquid* reserves, which are required only against any part of the total likely to be withdrawn at short notice. It is also unnecessary to hold *international* reserves to meet all withdrawals since the balances will be largely utilised for payments to the United Kingdom.

On the 1962 figures at any rate the crude formulation of the ratio so long accepted is clearly invalid. A ratio of the order known to exist in that year should suffice for crisis needs: in 1964 a credit of £1000 million was enough to stop a run on sterling. If the full extent of the reserves had been realised, speculation against the pound would have been much less likely and fluctuations in the trade balance could have been met without undue strain.

This points to the confidence factor in the broadest sense. Twenty years ago sterling was naturally rated as weak: the dollar at that time seemed impregnable and its status to some extent accentuated the inevitable weakness of the pound. War strains and losses were, however, unjustifiably magnified and this attitude persisted long after it should have been discarded: it was supported by constant references to the allegedly endemic deficit in the current balance; the belief that the United Kingdom as a debtor country was insolvent; and the fictitious reserve ratio commonly accepted. All these statements conflict with the evidence.

The Treasury told the Radcliffe Committee that the maintenance of confidence in sterling was a major policy objective. In retrospect it is hard to see that much was done by the authorities to provide the data on which confidence could reasonably be based. A recent crisis exemplifies the

[1] In 1965 it was announced that these securities were to be 'liquefied'.

results of this failure: the Bank of England has estimated that in 1964 approximately half the loss of reserves was due to the confidence factor.

With confidence reasonably assured a case can be made for meeting emergencies by freely drawing on the reserves rather than by counter-crisis measures but the practicability of such a policy depends largely on the size of the reserves.

Experience elsewhere is instructive. The record for the United States shows that although a massive reserve (25 billion dollars) cannot give absolute security, it does allow time for a brief crisis to subside or for remedial measures to be taken: since 1958 the United States has lost more than 10 billion dollars in gold but this loss has been spread over a number of years. The lesson for the United Kingdom is plain. So long as sterling remains a key-currency, large-scale withdrawals from the reserves may occur, even when the economy is sound: if the events of the 1960s are to be taken as typical, a short-term capital efflux amounting to some £500 million within a few months may be encountered.

Under such conditions it is clear that for the United Kingdom as for the United States absolute security by means of a very large reserve is unattainable: it seems equally clear that if heavy periodic losses occur, one policy objective should be to reinforce the reserves. The analysis presented here suggests that it may not be easy to do so.

The practical difficulty of securing an increase in the total should now be apparent. The obstacles may be listed as follows.

First, it is unlikely that a current surplus will add to the reserves. Despite continued emphasis since the war on the need to expand hard-currency earnings, the United Kingdom has almost invariably been in deficit with the non-sterling world.

Secondly, it no longer seems possible (as it once was) for the overseas sterling area to replenish the pool from earnings of non-sterling currency: in this sector the current balance has for years been in deficit.

Thirdly, the reserves may rise if the aggregate deficit

(current account) of the whole sterling area is offset by imports of long-term capital from non-sterling countries. Such an inflow is not amenable to United Kingdom policy (except in so far as net receipts may be increased by restrictions on capital exports to non-sterling countries) and can be checked by United States policy.

Finally, an attempt may be made to attract short-term capital. This also is not readily amenable to policy measures: high interest rates are usually impotent where confidence is lacking. Moreover, short-term funds, because of their volatile character, constitute a very unstable element in the reserves.

Of these four factors, only the first is directly dependent on the state of the United Kingdom economy and the others are, in the main, exempt from control by the United Kingdom Government. Such conditions clearly limit the scope of policy.

The evidence reviewed in the present chapter may now permit some general conclusions on the role of capital movements in the working of the sterling system. The capital account no less than the current account appears as an essential factor in the post-war problem: it concerns not merely the United Kingdom's creditor status but topics such as the sterling balances and the reserves. Each topic involves also the capital account of overseas sterling countries since they participate in the central reserves through capital as well as current transactions while their own reserves (the sterling balances) are now (like the central reserves) mainly dependent on capital flows.

A full appraisal along these lines reveals the relatively minor role of the United Kingdom's current balance in under-pinning sterling. It was not the cumulative surplus but the long-term capital inflow which sustained the reserves during the 1950s; the surplus was likewise ineffective as an agent for reducing the sterling balances since it was neutralised by capital imports into overseas sterling countries. Similarly, during the 1960s, the efflux of short-term capital was more potent than the current deficit in depleting the reserves. Further reactions can be envisaged: a check to the sterling area's imports of capital might not only reduce the reserves but, if it also reduced the balances of overseas sterling countries, the resulting exchange stringency would soon affect United Kingdom exports.

This possibility exemplifies the inter-dependence of the two main balance of payments categories: in a period of heavy capital movements it may be easier to connect the capital account with the current balance than to relate the latter to variations in reserves or liabilities. Capital exports themselves tend to create a trade surplus while the reverse is true of capital imports; in addition, the former will expand and the latter restrict invisible receipts. Thus, while an export surplus can be appropriated for overseas investment (and is often deemed an essential prerequisite) it is also likely that the investment itself will help to create the surplus needed.

Finally, it is clear that the capital account itself is highly complex. The data which have come under review here concern not the United Kingdom alone but other countries also: they cover both imports and exports of capital, on private and on Government account: these again can be classed as either short-term or long-term, and the long-term element further broken down into portfolio and direct investment. There is thus a parallel with the current account: just as the latter includes such diverse categories as visible trade, the normal or traditional invisible items, and the novel item for Government expenditure, so the former comprises a number of categories which differ not only in name but in character. Since in either case an over-simplified approach must be unrealistic and can hardly prove effective, analysis and policy should allow for this diversity. The post-war record suggests that failure to do so may well have contributed to the persistence of the sterling problem.

CHAPTER FIVE

The Problem in Perspective

The main elements of the post-war sterling problem have now been identified. The behaviour of the current balance has been recorded (Chapter Two) and analysed (Chapter Three): the material for this category has been supplemented by a statement of the capital account (Chapter Four). Any firm appraisal of the problem must be based on the data presented in these chapters.

Resurvey of the data yields the following preliminary results:

i. The United Kingdom has balanced its current account. Claims that the country has been 'unable to pay its way' should be checked against the record. Omitting the 1940s (when post-war recovery was still in progress) there was a cumulative balance of over £1000 million for the 1950s followed by a cumulative deficit of under £500 million for the first quinquennium of the 1960s.

ii. The net surplus for the 15 years since 1950 was earned despite large debits for Defence and Aid: these new burdens should be specified when evaluating the results. The deficit for 1960–64 is struck after debiting £1800 million on Government account: the commercial surplus for the quinquennium was £1300 million.

iii. On capital account, with overseas investments more than twice as great as before the war, the United Kingdom is again a creditor country, showing a substantial net surplus of assets. The liabilities created during the war have been mostly repaid but post-war capital movements have created new liabilities: these involve (as the wartime balances did not) a large annual debit on investment account. Disclosed reserves, only £600 million at the beginning of the 1950s, rose to approximately £1000 million in the 1960s.[1]

The results do not reveal any persistent or exceptional weakness in the balance of payments and the structure of the current account hardly suggests that it is now more vulnerable than formerly. It has been fortified not only by making good war losses but also by progressive expansion of the major credits: with export volume twice as great as before the war (and a much smaller increase for imports) the visible trade balance has been strengthened. Net invisibles on private account at approximately £600 million are in monetary terms more than twice the pre-war figure: receipts from overseas investment, always the main credit in this category, have increased threefold. Only the large Government debit has proved intractable although the new debit on investment account is also troublesome. On the whole the results for the purely economic categories may be regarded as good and weakness can be imputed only in so far as they are offset by an ever-rising total of Government expenditure.

The capital account has also been reinforced. Recovery of creditor status has eliminated a major weakness and as the reserves can now be proved much larger than was formerly believed, the reserve ratio seems adequate. It may also be noted that despite successive crises the reserves (in dollar terms) have been maintained at about the end-war figure.

This appraisal can be further tested by relating recent results to the long-term trend and by a comparison with the results for other countries. On either basis there is little

[1] It is true that in 1965 the level of the reserves was sustained by borrowing from the IMF and the United States. But the same is true of the United States reserves which in the early 1960s were sustained by inducing foreign central banks to build up balances in New York: the IMF has estimated (*Annual Report*, 1965) that for the preceding six years as a whole the United States had financed 40 per cent of its deficit in this way. The extent of the borrowing became apparent when France withdrew its excess balances in 1965, repatriating nearly 1 billion dollars.

reason to rate the record for the United Kingdom as poor or its balance of payments as specially vulnerable.

In historic retrospect the record compares better than is often supposed. It is sometimes assumed that during the years of 19th-century prosperity the current balance was invariably buoyant, with a surplus far above any which could now be envisaged. The reality was otherwise. For the years 1866–80 the surplus averaged less than £50 million per annum and although during the 1880s it was as high as £75 million, the average was again under £50 million in the 1890s and early 1900s.[1] When allowance is made for price changes it can be said that save for the debit on Government account (unknown a hundred years ago) there has been no long-term deterioration in the current balance (if the Government debit be deemed evidence of deterioration it should be recognised that the United States balance of payments has deteriorated similarly). Equally unfounded is the notion that there were formerly heavy exports of capital: on the contrary it is now evident that as compared with recent years 19th-century capital exports were relatively small.

The trend for visible trade is frequently quoted in this context, the secular decline for the United Kingdom share of world exports being taken as evidence of underlying weakness. This decline, however, has produced no adverse effects since it has been associated with a large increase in the volume of exports: by the end of the 1920s the index for export volume was some 30 per cent higher than at the beginning of the century and thirty years later recorded a two-fold increase. The likelihood that the increase was dependent on a wider distribution of world exports should not be overlooked.

The general conclusion suggested by such data can be supported by putting the problem in a wider setting and comparing the United Kingdom balance of payments with that of countries such as the United States or the members of the European Economic Community.

[1] Figures from A. H. Imlah: *Economic Elements in the Pax Britannica* (Harvard University Press, 1958).

The United Kingdom comes well out of the first comparison. Its record for exports is relatively favourable: although in the later 1950s both countries failed to maintain their share of world trade, the volume of United Kingdom exports rose by 28 per cent between 1953 and 1960 as against an increase of only 21 per cent for the United States: during this period the United Kingdom also increased its share of the market in Canada and Latin America (both dominated by the United States) and can thus be considered as fully competitive with the latter country. In some respects the record presents contrasts. The United States (unlike the United Kingdom) was able to create a large export surplus but the deficit for the basic balance (current and long-term capital transactions) was immensely greater for the former country:[1] the United Kingdom was able to maintain its reserves while the United States (though aided by huge borrowings from central banks) lost nearly half its gold. Taking the evidence as a whole it could perhaps be said that compared with the United States (normally considered a dynamic and efficient economy) the United Kingdom performance was good.

During recent years, however, criticism of the United Kingdom has mainly centred on its performance relative to the members of the European Economic Community: more specifically, it was claimed that these countries had been able to secure rapid growth without inflation and without generating balance of payments deficits. Such a view is no longer tenable. While the growth rate for the Community was exceptionally rapid, there is now clear evidence that it occasioned severe inflation: for 1963–64 the deficit on trade account averaged over £1000 million per annum (the corresponding figure for the United Kingdom was £300 million). Here again the comparison is by no means unfavourable: despite allegedly superior efficiency, the Community was clearly unable to balance its accounts. Even

[1] For the period 1958–64 the basic deficit for the United States was 15 billion dollars; for the United Kingdom 3 billion dollars.

Germany, so long presented as a model, incurred a deficit in 1965.[1]

The international comparisons may help to determine in what sense the cumulative deficit for the first quinquennium of the 1960s marked a deterioration after the cumulative surplus of the 1950s. As already seen (pp. 60–1) unit costs developed favourably for the United Kingdom: this in itself should have reinforced the trade balance and can perhaps be related to the emergence of an adverse balance for the Common Market countries. The simultaneous emergence of the United States deficit also eased the problem of dollar supplies (largely through long-term capital flows). In such an environment any relative weakness in the United Kingdom balance of payments would be unlikely and seems inconsistent with the data: despite two exceptionally bad years for the trade balance, the average surplus of over £250 million per annum on private account hardly suggests failure of the economy. With the deficit wholly on Government account, the result represented primarily a twofold increase in Government expenditure overseas as compared with the preceding quinquennium.

On this record it seems necessary to ask whether the sterling problem really exists. Reference to wartime losses is no longer realistic as these have been made good: the dollar shortage disappeared in the closing years of the 1950s; inflation is largely irrelevant, given the evidence for inflationary pressures elsewhere. Yet the balance of payments is still a controversial issue. The main targets of criticism are as follows.

First, the visible trade account is said to be unsatisfactory: imports as well as exports are held responsible for faulty performance by the trade balance.

The case here remains unproved. As already seen, a declining share in world trade is no proof that exports are uncompetitive and it need not denote weakness since the operative factor is the volume of exports at any one time.

[1] The current deficit for 1965 exceeded £600 million, 50 per cent more than the United Kingdom deficit in 1964.

Such a trend can be (as recently in the United States) compatible with an increasingly favourable trade balance or (as in the United Kingdom, long-term and short-term) associated with a great expansion of export volume. If during recent years Germany and other European countries had not secured an increasing share of world exports, they would have been unable to offer (as now) a large market for United Kingdom exports: similarly, on a long-term view, the fall in the United Kingdom share of world trade can be interpreted as essential for a continued rise in exports.

Adverse criticism of the trend for imports seems likewise unfounded. Heavy imports in a particular year may be traced to stock-building but it is also asserted that large imports of manufactures prove that British goods are non-competitive even in the home market. Again, the evidence must be regarded as unconvincing since such imports constitute a much smaller proportion of total imports than is the case in many European countries. Furthermore, the assertion is inconsistent with the longer-term trend for relative movements of exports and imports: in a country like the United Kingdom heavily dependent on imports of food and raw materials as well as on certain manufactures, a twofold increase for export volume with only a 30 per cent increase for imports registers efficiency.

It is thus not easy to detect weakness in the trade account, especially as the data do not indicate gross disequilibrium: in good years there has been a near-balance and even in bad years the import surplus has been far below the pre-war average revalued at current prices.[1] It has also to be remembered that the trade balance cannot be considered in isolation. The United Kingdom formerly accepted a large import surplus as normal; the United States now has a huge export surplus and also a balance of payments deficit; the

[1] A fact which must also weaken the claim that the deficit is the result of over-full employment. Viewed in perspective even the import surplus for 1964 (£550 million) does not seem excessive. In 1938 the comparable figure was £300 million which at present prices would amount to about £1000 million: no one could claim that the import surplus registered over-full employment in 1938.

enormous deficit for the Common Market countries (despite a rising share of world trade) is not commonly interpreted as a symptom of basic weakness. As evidence, therefore, the trade balance taken by itself is unreliable.

An even more frequent criticism is the recurrence of crises, which are supposed to register chronic failure. But this view is suspect also. Post-war crises were very diverse in character and it would be unjustifiable to infer consistently poor performance on the part of the United Kingdom.

The contrast noted earlier (pp. 18–19) between crises in the current balance and crises occasioned by losses of reserves is suggestive here. In the first place it must raise doubts whether any one theory can explain the problem of sterling: more probably different factors create different types of crisis. Secondly, it narrows down to very few cases the crises which can be ascribed to an inefficient economy. For the majority (the reserve crises) the drain on the reserves represented demands by the overseas sterling area or non-sterling countries: in other words, these crises derived from external rather than internal factors. Finally (of special relevance for policy-making), it rebuts the claim that growth reveals weakness in the current balance: during an entire decade (1950–59) this could not have been true on more than one occasion at most.

On the whole it would appear that the susceptibility of the current balance to crisis has been over-emphasised: post-war strains were not for the most part occasioned by weakness in this sector and were thus only indirectly (if at all) a reflection of domestic trends. The conclusion corroborates the evidence which suggests that the current balance is not now more vulnerable than formerly and a more extended survey would provide further corroboration by showing that crises are not a novel phenomenon. Even during the period of 19th-century prosperity (when the balance of payments was indisputably sound) external strains marked by a loss of reserves recurred from time to time: in fact the gold standard technique was developed by the Bank of England to counteract such crises.

When the problem is placed in an international setting, the impact of crises looks less severe: it could hardly be claimed that the United Kingdom is unique in this respect. The dollar no less than the pound has long been under pressure and comparable strains can be found in many other cases: these include not merely developing countries (such as India, Pakistan and Ceylon in the sterling area) but those at a more advanced stage of development such as Japan and Canada, Australia and New Zealand while balance of payments crises have always been endemic in Latin America. More recently, too, the Common Market countries (generally rated as highly efficient) have succumbed in the same way.

Even a cursory review, therefore, does not confirm the suggestion that the United Kingdom is specially liable to crisis: its experience is common elsewhere. The Brookings Report on the United States balance of payments emphasised that the *main* conclusion to be drawn from post-war history was the likelihood of large annual changes.[1] During the 1950s the United States actually incurred a deficit on current account in 1953 and 1959: this record was no better than that of the United Kingdom, which also lapsed into deficit on two occasions (1951 and 1955). Again, during the first quinquennium of the 1960s the Common Market countries (popularly supposed to have attained growth without inflation) were heavily in deficit on trade account in 1963 and 1964: this record was similarly comparable with that of the United Kingdom, also heavily in deficit for visible trade in two years (1960 and 1964). As already seen, the impact of crisis on the reserves was less severe in the United Kingdom than in the United States: it could also be maintained that in other ways sterling stood up better to post-war strains than some other currencies. France, for example, though said to be highly dynamic, devalued the franc in the 1940s and again in the 1950s while in the early 1960s it was once more in danger.

Yet another target for criticism is the level of the reserves.

[1] *The US Balance of Payments in 1968* (US Govt Printing Office, Washington, 1963), p. 12.

It is usually held that at approximately £1000 million they are embarrassingly low as that figure allows insufficient scope for absorbing a deficit in the current balance or an efflux of short-term capital: furthermore, inadequate reserves not only cause practical inconvenience but also adversely affect confidence. Although it has long been a major policy objective to increase the total, only limited progress has been made towards this objective during the past fifteen years.

Expressed in these terms the case is misleading. As is now known, the official figures grossly understate the amount actually available for use in case of need and even if since the war there has been no large increase in the total, the United Kingdom, despite successive crises, has maintained the reserves at the end-war level (the United States, with a much stronger economy, has in recent years failed notably in this respect). It should also be emphasised that the level of the reserves is not determined by the United Kingdom balance of payments alone.

Although it is often claimed that the reserves actually available are far from adequate, in historic retrospect they can hardly be considered small. Not much more than a hundred years ago the Bank of England worked with a reserve of about £10 million (which was sometimes reduced to £3 million under crisis conditions). At the outbreak of World War I the total was only £38 million and at the return to the gold standard in 1925 no more than £150 million. There was little increase before the gold standard was abandoned in 1931. Such comparisons do not support the view that the present figure is unusually low.

As an indicator of weakness the reserve position thus proves as unreliable as the recurrence of crises or the behaviour of the trade balance. This conclusion points to the need for accurate diagnosis before policy is formulated. After debate extending over twenty years there is still no consensus of opinion on even the core of the problem or the best evidence of its impact.

To some extent faulty diagnosis has been due to poor documentation. A major instance was the failure to assess the United Kingdom's debtor status at the end of the war: it was not until 1964 that an official estimate showed the country as a substantial net creditor, with quick reserves more than twice the total hitherto known. But even the data available were frequently neglected and it was rarely recognised that British conditions were not exceptional. As late as 1950, when receipts from overseas investments were known to be greater than before the war, ministerial statements claimed that all overseas investments had been lost.[1] There were constant assertions (against the weight of the evidence) that inflation had made exports non-competitive or that the trade deficit was due to an inefficient economy (a test often applied to Britain but seldom applied elsewhere). Similarly, any loss of reserves was taken as evidence of fundamental disequilibrium in the United Kingdom but not in the United States.

Perhaps the main diagnostic error was the failure to appreciate the intricacy of the problem. Over-simplification of the issues was apparent in discussion of the current balance as if it were merely the trade balance assumed in classical analysis without allowing for the novel debits on Government account which were equally relevant, in magnitude sometimes greater, and usually immune from economic controls. Just as misleading was the over-simplification involved in the failure to allow for the working of the sterling system with (for example) the unreal assumption that movements in the reserves reflected only the trend for the United Kingdom's current balance. Such an approach omits essential factors which should be included in a full diagnosis: these can only be identified by a comprehensive survey of the total balance of payments as it developed after the war.

The conclusion is applicable to a concrete case. Inspection of the record will show the basic flaw in diagnosing inflation as the root of the trouble: the diagnosis fails because the new

[1] 'We have to face the loss of all our overseas investments. We now have to pay by the current products of this country for all the goods we require.' (The Home Secretary, Mr J. Chuter Ede, as reported in *Hansard*, 7 November 1950, col. 817.)

balance of payments structure allows only limited scope for the operation of inflationary forces. Such forces acting primarily on the trade balance (and on little else in the current account) are irrelevant to certain categories which have latterly become especially prominent, e.g. the Government debit, capital flows, and movements in the reserves attributable to the overseas sterling area. With all these operative on a significant scale, the balance of payments mechanism which has now evolved cannot function in the same way as a relatively simple model with a predictable response from inflation or deflation.

An agreed diagnosis is only the first step in policy-making: when it has been finalised, the objectives of policy must be stated and decisions taken as to the methods by which these objectives are to be attained.

The complications which make diagnosis so risky will recur in any attempt to define objectives. On the evidence it is clearly inadequate to aim at a large increase in exports, a greater share of world trade or even a massive surplus on trade account: the post-war record for the United Kingdom, the European Economic Community and the United States, respectively, proves that none of these will guarantee security. In the United Kingdom even a substantial cumulative surplus on current account has been insufficient while heavy overseas investments and the recovery of creditor status have failed to bring immunity from trouble. Again, when it is proposed that the main policy objective should be to accumulate reserves to a figure which would enable crises to be surmounted without strain, the proposal should be tested by reference to specific cases: United States experience shows that even a huge reserve is of limited value as a safeguard since it can be depleted very rapidly while the same is true of the enormous assets held by India at the end of the war.

The point can be elaborated by examining one specific objective: a surplus on current account. Without discussing the size of the surplus which would be considered adequate, the implications of the proposal may be listed:

i. Such a surplus is unlikely to replenish the reserves: the current balance has since the war been in deficit with the non-sterling world (except in 1950 and 1953 when imports were tightly restricted).

ii. A surplus will probably (*ceteris paribus*) reduce the London balances of the overseas sterling area. This may have harmful repercussions for the United Kingdom itself as well as for the countries primarily concerned.

iii. A surplus will not eliminate crises: twice within ten years (1949 and 1957) crises emerged although the current balance was not in deficit.

iv. The notion that an inadequate surplus will imperil growth assumes that growth must expose weakness in the current balance. Post-war history does not bear out such a view.

v. There is little substance in the claim that a surplus is needed to cover overseas investment in order to guard against a drain on the reserves: pressure on the reserves comes not from long-term investment in non-sterling countries (which is controlled) but from short-term outflows (which are uncontrolled).

vi. A surplus will not necessarily maintain confidence. In July 1965 confidence failed although the trade deficit for the preceding six months had been cut by one-half and the latest estimates (for January–March) showed that the deficit on current account had disappeared.

With these limitations it would be rash to conclude that the creation of a surplus would solve the problem of sterling (point iii) or would even help by increasing the reserves (point i) or sustaining confidence (point vi); it could be harmful (point ii) and seems unnecessary (points iv and v). Insistence on a current surplus may thus be a policy error comparable to insistence on a budget surplus as the prior essential for recovery in the early 1930s.

Once the objective has been chosen, the next step in the formulation of policy is the choice of the means by which it is to be attained. If (despite the objections listed above) the current balance is to be reinforced and if devaluation and deflation are ruled out as either harmful or ineffective (and an incomes policy as impracticable or useless) the main policies available are measures to raise the efficiency of the economy or to step up the growth rate.

With the former, although the case for efficiency is undeniable, the effects on the balance of payments are likely to appear (if at all) in the longer-term and even a high degree of efficiency may not produce the desired result. In this respect the United Kingdom economy has since the war been compared unfavourably first with the United States and later with the Common Market: nevertheless, the allegedly superior efficiency of these economies (whether exemplified in technological progress, competitive price levels or general dynamism) has not protected them from balance of payments strains. There is thus reason to doubt the value of a policy aimed at increasing efficiency as a remedy for the problem of sterling.

A similar conclusion seems justified where reliance is placed on growth as a solution. Such a policy assumes that with steady growth in the economy the current balance would develop favourably. Recent experience abroad lends no support to such a view: in the Common Market the expectations so often claimed for it have not been fulfilled while in the United States the deficit appeared just as the economy entered a phase of rapid growth in 1958. For the United Kingdom itself two detailed appraisals have been made which on this point are unanimous. Estimates prepared by the National Economic Development Council[1] could not envisage after a period of uninterrupted growth (and restricted incomes) more than an approximate balance of exports and imports (a balance already attained at the end of the 1950s and again in 1962–63): a similar result is forecast for 1970 in the recent Five-Year Plan.[2] If these estimates are valid, the realisation of a current surplus depends on the doubtful contingency of a favourable trend for invisibles.

[1] NEDC: *Growth of the UK Economy to 1966* (HMSO, 1963).
[2] Cmnd. 2764: *The National Plan* (HMSO, 1965).

The case can be restated in another way. On the assumption that import restriction (by direct or indirect means) is unacceptable, policies aimed at growth and efficiency (like deflation and devaluation) only repeat the policy of export expansion put forward at the end of the war. It remains to ask whether this policy in a new form will be more successful than hitherto. The record does not imply that for the post-war period as a whole the crucial issue was the failure of exports: does the solution lie in a further expansion?

To question whether long-term policy should be based solely on export expansion (or an increase in the efficiency of the economy designed to generate a larger volume of exports) is not to question the role of exports in the current balance or the need for industrial efficiency but merely to emphasise that the balance of payments includes items other than visible trade and to suggest that neglect of this fact may vitiate policy in the future as in the past.

It is perhaps significant that no target figure has been fixed for the proposed expansion. At the end of the war it was thought that a 75 per cent increase in export volume as compared with pre-war would be sufficient; at the end of the 1950s policy was framed on the assumption that exports should rise to an extent sufficient to yield a current surplus of £300–400 million. On the latter basis the approach was more realistic in that it allowed for the possibility of an increase in exports being nullified by an opposite trend for the invisibles but the degree of export expansion needed to create the required surplus is still indeterminate.

The issue can be clarified by setting the trend for visible trade against the trend for invisibles: it then becomes obvious that *no* specific increase in exports will be adequate if offset by a deterioration elsewhere. To accept such a deterioration as inevitable or irreversible and to postulate that exports must rise sufficiently to counter this trend raises a further question: is such an expansion practicable?

Post-war history may suggest an answer: on the record it seems doubtful whether exports can be indefinitely expanded to the extent needed. Apart from the data for the United

Kingdom itself (which show an enormous but inadequate increase in export volume) there is other evidence to the same effect: the United States deficit also exemplifies the risks of allowing an undue increase for invisible debits. If the United States, with immense resources and an almost impregnable balance of payments, has been unable to step up exports to the extent needed, it seems unlikely that the United Kingdom will be able to do so.

The comparison with the United States should perhaps be pursued to indicate the parallel between the pound and the dollar. The inherent strength of the United States balance of payments has proved insufficient for the burdens placed upon it: the basic problem for the United Kingdom is substantially the same. To say that the country has been unable to pay its way is no more true for the United Kingdom than it would be for the United States: even in 1964, with an exceptionally large trade deficit, there was a surplus for all commercial transactions in the current account and a deficit only when the huge Government debit is superimposed. For each country the problem is not merely to live within its income but to earn enough to meet commitments which are incurred largely on behalf of others.

Once this conclusion is accepted, it further exposes the weakness of a policy which fails to allow for a multiplicity of diverse factors. Measures aimed at export promotion (by deflation, devaluation or other means) not only neglect various possible sources of disequilibrium but also place an undue burden on the trade balance in seeking to effect readjustment by operating via one category alone. On both counts any policy which can cover only a limited front is likely to prove ineffective. A more comprehensive approach may be the first prerequisite for a fully-articulated policy.

Another prerequisite for policy-making is the provision of adequate data. Without a firm statistical basis the problem can be grossly misconceived: the misconceptions which arose at the end of the war continued for years to obscure the true nature of post-war strains. Discussion of the dollar problem was likewise hampered by the lack of reliable data which could serve as a check on the proposal to devalue the pound: on some tests at least it looked as if the dollar were equally suspect. Similarly, in balance of payments discussions during the 1950s the progress of inflation in the United Kingdom as compared with other countries was not readily measurable. It can hardly be doubted that if in each case full data had been available the debate would have been on a very different plane.

In recent years a good deal has been done to improve and extend the statistical material needed for policy-making. There are now reasonable estimates for the main components of the current balance; there are also detailed figures for capital movements and those for the sterling balances have been revised although the totals commonly used for the reserves are still misleading. The Bank of England has published authoritative data on overseas investments and the net creditor status of the United Kingdom.

Much more is needed. At several points in this study it has been found that no certain conclusion can be stated until the issues have been defined by further research.

The behaviour of the trade balance in particular is open to question. On the export side the competitive rating applicable to United Kingdom manufactures is still in doubt and perhaps data should be secured from an extended survey of the type carried out by the United States Department of Commerce for the period 1954–61.[1] This survey analysed exports in forty-four product groups for eight different regions, thus testing competitiveness in three hundred and fifty-two regional product markets. Despite the smaller United States share of world trade, the study failed to reveal any general decline in competitiveness as measured in this way. If as a result of a similar survey United Kingdom exports were found to be fully competitive with those of other countries, the notion that cost-inflation has upset the trade balance would be untenable.

A market survey might also expose a real weakness.

[1] Cf. summary of results in Brookings Report, pp. 65–8.

Although the overseas Commonwealth is one of the main outlets for United Kingdom exports (until the 1960s taking some 40 per cent) this trade has failed to expand in recent years: between 1955 and 1960, for example, the Commonwealth total was virtually unchanged while exports to the European Economic Community and the United States rose sharply. A detailed study would make clear the extent to which the Commonwealth market is restricted not only by tariffs but also by prohibitions, quotas or exchange controls: where these exist, any attempt to increase exports by lowering prices will be frustrated. Even where access to the market is relatively unrestricted, local protectionism is often so strong that the attempt can have harmful reactions if lower prices constitute a threat to domestic producers: in Canada, for example, anti-dumping duties are applied to United Kingdom goods (in other words, the export prices of these goods are not too high but too low). Thus over a broad sector[1] a policy aimed at making exports more competitive is liable to be self-defeating.

A comprehensive study of the trade sector should thus cover not merely exports but also commercial policy. The contrast between the buoyancy of the United States visible balance and the more sensitive United Kingdom balance may be partly due to differences in economic structure but certain aspects of policy may be relevant also. The Free Trade tradition in the United Kingdom contrasts with the Protectionist tradition in the United States: only a full study would show how far each has been modified. Moreover, in the United Kingdom there are non-commercial factors which probably work with special force against the creation of a trade surplus: these would include unilateral concessions to under-developed countries or a bias in favour of the Commonwealth under the preferential system (including

[1] The United States is another country where controls can be (and are) invoked when imports become too competitive. Magnitudes again: the United States is now the largest individual market for United Kingdom exports while Canada accounted for one-half of the total adverse trade balance in 1964.

here not merely tariffs but price preferences, restrictions on competitive imports, etc.).

Such factors may govern the trade balance to a greater extent than is generally realised. The record for Germany as well as the United States deserves attention. The favourable German trade balance in recent years has usually been attributed to highly competitive exports: much less weight has been given to commercial policy on the import side. A recent study[1] has made it clear that the reality was very different: import restrictions (especially for foodstuffs and fuels) largely accounted for the persistent surplus on visible trade.

The analytical study of exports and imports could be supplemented by comparative data on the intensity of inflationary pressures in the United Kingdom and elsewhere. In this context the behaviour of the United States trade balance is of special interest. In 1946 Keynes forecast weakness in the balance as a result of trends already apparent: this view was based on the assumption that in the United States economy certain fundamental forces tend to restrict the development of any large surplus on trade account. As envisaged by Keynes:

> There are in these matters deep undercurrents at work, natural forces one can call them, or even the invisible hand, which are operating towards equilibrium. . . . The United States is becoming a high-living, high-cost country beyond any previous experience.[2]

The failure of this forecast did not pass unnoticed during the earlier post-war years when the dollar shortage was acute. Those who accepted the Keynesian view explained that it referred to longer-term trends: in 1951 Harrod claimed[3] that it could not properly be tested on the basis of experience until a decade had elapsed but even now, much later, there is no sign of the forecast being justified. During

[1] J. Markus: *Some Observations on the West German Trade Surplus* (Oxford Economic Papers, March 1965).

[2] *Economic Journal*, June 1946.

[3] R. F. Harrod: *Life of J. M. Keynes* (Macmillan, 1951), p. 621.

the 1930s the favourable trade balance of the United States was less than 500 million dollars per annum (say, 1·5 billion at present prices): by the early 1950s it averaged 2 billion and in the early 1960s was as much as 5 billion. Even allowing for exports tied to Aid, this must be rated a highly buoyant surplus instead of the deficit expected.[1]

On these results the doctrine of inflationary pressure as a limitation on the development of the trade surplus (at least in the form stated by Keynes) is untenable. The implications for the United Kingdom should perhaps be investigated. A new view of the trade balance might well emerge from study of the process which in the United States generates a massive (and constantly rising) export surplus despite high wages, the pressure of demand and a declining share of world exports.

Further work is also needed on the invisible items and especially on the repercussions of Government expenditure overseas. It should not be impracticable to estimate how far such expenditure affects exports: an estimate of this kind is available for the United States. On the other side of the account a figure for Government imports (not at present shown separately) should be published in order to reveal the full magnitude of the Government debit. Other possible interrelationships between the trade balance and current invisibles could perhaps be usefully explored, e.g. to see whether (as is sometimes claimed) the return on direct investment in the United Kingdom is offset by exports attributable to such investment. A detailed comparison of the return on the United Kingdom's overseas investments with the return on foreign investment in the United Kingdom should also prove informative in assessing the costs and benefits of foreign investment.

Similar studies should help in the evaluation of the capital account. Here the prime need is to trace the impact of capital flows on the trade balance. The assumption that capital exports normally stimulate visible exports may need

[1] A recent estimate by the Department of Commerce envisages a further increase to almost 10 billion dollars by 1970.

modification in so far as overseas investment is now (as formerly it was not) largely concerned with the industrialisation of countries which are the main markets for United Kingdom manufactures. On the other hand it is conceivable that the buoyancy of the United States trade balance may owe much to massive investment overseas: a comparative study would perhaps reveal significant contrasts with the United Kingdom. An attempt should also be made to gauge the net impact of capital imports. The initial impact on the reserves in the form of capital receipts is traceable but may soon be offset by heavy service payments and the eventual result may be a debit. The result would in any case have to be related to the secondary impact on the visible trade sector.

Rehearsal of these particulars serves to define the scope of a study which would cover the whole complex of international economic relations: not merely the trade balance and current invisibles but also capital flows (long-term and short-term) in either direction; when seeking the origins of disequilibrium the analysis will not be confined to economic forces but will allow for political factors (which may operate on the current or the capital account) and the confidence factor (which may likewise produce repercussions on either). In this way it should be possible to show how the balance of payments mechanism actually works.

The value of such a study lies in its practical applications: it can be utilised to test theories and policies. The detail for the current account may now suggest that there has been undue emphasis on the behaviour of the trade balance while insufficient attention has been given to the role of the invisible items although the latter exerted a potent if unobtrusive influence. A broader survey would also question the emphasis as between the current account and the capital account: policy has been mostly aimed at the former although crucial factors operate in the latter. Here again the detail is relevant: long-term capital flows are in fact largely innocuous while short-term movements cause crises. On such tests it must seem at least doubtful whether policy should be mainly concerned with the trade balance to the virtual exclusion of other items in the current account or with exports of long-term capital but not short-term capital outflows.

With this approach there will also be reservations on any diagnosis which bases the trend for sterling primarily on the performance of the United Kingdom economy: a realistic study reveals the presence of forces other than those compendiously termed inflation or deflation. Although the trade balance is responsive to the state of the economy, the magnitude of the Government debit is determined by non-economic factors; capital movements will be largely occasioned by conditions abroad or decisions taken elsewhere; the trade balance itself may reflect commercial policies adopted for political reasons. The significance of these reactions will be great if the United Kingdom is unusually vulnerable on such points. The Government debit, for example, is likely to be specially onerous if not offset by concomitant exports; the trade balance likewise may be sensitive to policies which are biased in favour of external interests.

To specify a number of diverse forces as determinants of the total balance is not to claim any exceptional status for the United Kingdom: on the contrary, the record for other countries is directly comparable. Long-term capital exports from the United States as well as short-term outflows have reduced its reserves while in France capital imports brought an accumulation of reserves. The confidence factor underlying short-term capital movements has been prominent not only in the United States and the United Kingdom but also in Germany, where it has helped to swell the reserves. The political factor expressed in the Government debit underlay the deficit in the United States as well as in the United Kingdom while in Germany receipts under this head contributed to the surplus. In all cases major reactions on the balance of payments originated not in the trade account but in other categories. Such an environment must impair the validity of analyses or policies which are concerned mainly with visible trade or the current balance in an obsolete form.

A final comparison may be ventured. In the United States (which as a key-currency country affords the closest parallel) the balance of payments problem has (as in the United Kingdom) proved intractable: despite the great inherent strength of the American economy, the deficit has for years resisted remedial measures. This may imply that the problem of sterling will not readily be solved, especially as it has not yet been possible to work out an agreed diagnosis. Such a view would accord with the interpretation presented in this study. But even if no full solution can be found, the analysis may at least expose the complexity of the problem and the irrelevance of any diagnosis which neglects the evidence.[1]

[1] Cf. the latest official diagnosis: 'We are trying to maintain an exceedingly liberal import policy built up in the 19th century in circumstances where the high overseas investment income associated with it has been sharply cut down by the two world wars' (Mr Douglas Jay, President of the Board of Trade, as reported in the *Financial Times*, 24 June 1965). In fact receipts from overseas investments are now at least three times as great as before World War I or World War II.

Index

Printed in Great Britain by Richard Clay (The Chaucer Press), Ltd., Bungay, Suffolk